DATA
HERDING

Copyright © 2021 by Keith Wood. All rights reserved.

No part of this publication may be reproduced, stored in a retrieval system, or transmitted in any form or by any means, electronic, mechanical, photocopying, recording, scanning, or otherwise, without the prior written permission of the author.

ISBN: 978-1-7365700-2-9 (paperback)
978-1-7365700-0-5 (e-book)

Cover design by	Klassic Designs (via the 99 Designs website)
	Cover design has been designed using resources from Freepik.com
Edited by	Jo Finchen-Parsons
	Thanks to Jo Finchen-Parsons, via Reedsy, for looking through this and making it better. https://reedsy.com/#/freelancers/jo-f
Interior layout by	Olivier Darbonville

Printed in the United States of America

DATA HERDING

THE ART OF EDI

KEITH WOOD

> **CONTENTS**

ABOUT THE AUTHOR **7**

ABOUT THE BOOK **9**

1. STANDARDS **13**
2. ENCRYIPTION AND SECURITY **21**
3. INTERFACING TO THE CUSTOMER **45**
4. PROCESSING **55**
5. MONITORING **73**
6. EMAILS AND ALERTS **83**
7. BOUNDARIES **91**
8. COMMON PITFALLS **97**
9. THE REASON FOR CONSISTENCY **107**
10. PEOPLE, PLACES, AND THINGS **111**

APPENDIX **125**

> ABOUT THE AUTHOR

My name is Keith Wood and I came of age a little before the internet became a thing. I feel I made the right call and got a degree in computer science in the early eighties (I was wavering between computer science and wildlife biology). I have been fortunate enough to remain employed in the technology sector since then. I'm not sure that I would call myself a geek or a nerd but I will admit that others do. My wife does. I do own a metal detector (two actually) and I like to use them on the beach.

Over the past thirty-five years I have worked in different industries and different roles. I have worked in both the manufacturing and the servicing sector. I have worked in the textile, pharmaceutical, and financial services industries. I have seen a lot of things, both good and bad, but I have never been bored. I have been exchanging data between different systems for most of my career. I believe that I have made many, if not all, of the mistakes that can be made when integrating systems. In this book I will take the lessons that I have learned from those mistakes and help you avoid them.

There are unique challenges when integrating your system with an external customer's system, which you may have no knowledge of. Most people who have never done this type of work can't really appreciate what has to be done. Integrating with a system which you have never seen can be difficult. Sometimes you have to try and crawl inside your trading partner's head to understand what they are seeing. Some of what we do can be frustrating but some of it can be entertaining as well.

I work with technology everyday yet I am still amazed on a regular basis by things I see people accomplishing with it - both helping and hurting our world.

> ABOUT
THE BOOK

THIS BOOK CONTAINS ALL THE lessons that I have learned over the years; lessons learned mainly by doing things the wrong way. In putting this together I hope to help people not repeat the same mistakes. I want this book to be relevant and useful for a long period of time, so I will stay away from making recommendations on what tools or systems you should purchase or use. Here, I am interested in sharing how to exchange data well, not how to carry out a particular task with a certain standard or on a specific platform. Advice on tools to use that is good today may not be so tomorrow and certainly will not be a few years from now.

This information should be helpful for anyone working in the EDI space; regardless if you are using a nice expensive third-party product with all the bells and whistles, or a bunch of shell scripts that you have hacked together over the years. I am trying to address challenges everyone is going to face and offer some potential solutions. More than anything I am trying to point out things you need to think about as you are interfacing with your external trading partners.

This book is not a deep dive into the complexities of the X12 standard and how purchase orders and invoices get generated and processed. Those things are beyond the scope of this book. This book will not walk you through step by step on mapping an 810 document into an XML format. There are many tools available and it would not be possible for me to cover all of the technical steps required to get each of them up and running. You will have to work through that part yourself.

Electronic Data Interchange (EDI) is what feeds data into, out of, and between systems - the plumbing of a software system, the grease that makes the wheels turn. EDI should be thought of as a utility just like the electricity in your home: you expect it to function in the background, providing what you need with minimal fuss. The greatest reward you can expect for doing a good job is to not be noticed. A lot of the time you will be working at the "base metal level" of a computer system. Some people like this kind of work, but there are also a lot that don't. You will probably work with people that have been assigned to your group that will not be happy about it and will be looking to get moved out as soon as possible.

I hear EDI referred to in ways that I don't agree. I hear that EDI applies to documents such as purchase orders, invoices, and other transactional documents. I have heard that EDI competes with XML, and that it competes with API's (Application Programming Interfaces). So, in this sense I believe people are viewing EDI as the same thing as the X12 standard. Even though there are other standards that compete with X12; EDIFACT and VDA for example.

In this book, to remain true to the purpose of helping readers employ best practices and avoid the many pitfalls I have experienced over the years, I have chosen to view EDI simply as what it name states; moving data back and forth between different systems, regardless of what the data looks like as it is being interchanged.

I do not see EDI as competing with XML. XML is just a way of formatting data when you are exchanging that data electronically with a business partner.

- *What EDI is:*
    - EDI will keep you engaged with your external customers.
    - EDI will allow you to have knowledge of most business processes within your organization.
    - EDI will allow you to take part with standard setting organizations, to the extent that you want.
    - EDI will allow you to fly under the radar (unless things go wrong).
    - EDI will get you blamed for a lot of things that you are not responsible for, nor that you have any control over.
    - EDI will allow you to be amazed by what your trading partners do at times.

- *What EDI is not:*
    - EDI is not something that is going to get you exposure to the latest and greatest technology frameworks.
    - It is not something that you can point to and say look at what I did.
    - It is not something that is going to bring you a lot of awards or recognition.

Let's get started with the foundation of any good data exchange; standards. When everyone uses them, life is wonderful.

01

> Although no one implements a standard in a standard way, starting with one and making specific necessary changes is far better than the chaos of using no standards at all.

>CHAPTER ONE
Standards

STANDARDS ARE GOOD. WHEN PEOPLE use standards, it is great. If people were to use standards in a standard way it would be Nirvana. Alas, Nirvana is a mythical place that doesn't really exist. There are a lot of people that put in a great deal of time and effort to develop standards to hopefully meet the needs of business. When these get turned loose in the wild, however, you will be amazed at how things actually get implemented.

I would like to give one example of something that I have personally had to deal with, where a standard was not used properly. I was implementing an interface with a major vendor in the mortgage industry. The standard that was being used was a good choice that had all of the data points defined. There just needed to be a way to transmit data about a new government program that had come out to help home owners who were underwater (owed more on their house than what it was actually worth). There was a data field already defined, implemented, and used throughout the industry to represent a mortgage insurance policy number. Instead of using that field to send the policy number, however, the vendor decided to send that critical piece of data in another field that was normally used to transmit the name of the system used to underwrite the loan. This was decided by the vendor within their development group with no discussions with any of their trading partners. Once announced there was no negotiating the decision. Making a change would have required the vendor to go back and do more development work which they were unwilling to do. Since they were such a major player in the industry there was no choice but to go back and create special logic, just for them, to map that data item. This was necessary work for all parties that were integrated with the vendor, which was everyone in the mortgage insurance industry.

I point this out because when you are implementing interfaces with your external trading partners, you can never know what to expect. The down side of this is that you will be incredulous at some of the things that you are forced to do that defies logic. The up side is that your work does not become boring, and eighteen years can slip by without you even noticing.

I don't want to get too far into the details about the different standards and standard bodies, but I do want to point out two major formats that you will see. XML and X12.

X12

Below is a snippet of a Mortgage Insurance Application in an X12 format. In "EDI language" this is called an 872 transaction set. This contains the address of a property that someone is requesting mortgage insurance on.

NX1?ZG?NX2?09?NY?NX2?07?BROOKLYN,?NX2?10?11203?NX2?15?794 JLA KLVZ LPJROHR 207?REA?31???04?04?1?????CY?2016?

XML

Below is the same Mortgage Insurance Application snippet in XML (eXtensible Markup Language) format.

```
<PROPERTY _StreetAddress="794 JLA KLVZ LPJ RQHR 207"
_City="BROOKLYN" _State="NY" _PostalCode="11203"
_FinancedNumberOfUnits="1" _StructureBuiltYear="2016"/>
```

The question marks in the X12 standard are actually special characters that do not represent themselves in a text document. You can see that the XML format is more readable and understandable to the human brain. There are other format standards, JSON and flat files among others. You and your trading partner will have to decide how to exchange data; do not skip this important step of communicating, and never assume a certain industry-specific standard, or even a standard, will be used. I strongly encourage you to choose a standard if there is one. The whole reason standards and standard bodies exists is to decrease the cost and complexity of doing business. Theoretically, once you have created an interface with one customer, if you are using a standard, then the cost of interfacing to the next customer is greatly reduced because you have already done most of the work.

Format vs Data

I need to point out that in my example above X12 and XML are a standard, and the data being transmitted is also a standard. The data being transmitted is a Mortgage Insurance Application. You can think of X12 and XML as the format standard, and the Mortgage Insurance Application as the data standard. There is a standards body that defines what X12 looks like (ASC X12), there is another standards body that defines what XML looks like (W3C), and there is yet another standards body that defines what a Mortgage Insurance Application looks like (MISMO). MISMO has defined what the Mortgage Insurance Application looks like using both the X12 and the XML format standards.

There could be some instances in which you may actually be on a conference call with a customer as well as your competitors. The customer may decide they want to build an interface with multiple businesses at once. Having a standard makes this possible. It can make for some awkward, but ultimately necessary, conversations. Assuming you are working in a business where a data standard exists, you and your competitors would have already had to collaborate in order to define what the standard is.

If you are lucky enough to participate in the discussions to create and maintain standards, you will want to make sure that you protect your business's interests and proprietary information, while at the same time making sure your data needs are met. Not only do you want to be a good steward for your business, but you also need to be careful not do to anything that could be considered as any type of collusion. I know this sounds pretty far-fetched, but if you are in a situation where you are discussing things with your competitors, it is something that you will need to be aware of. As a general rule you don't want to say anything about your internal processes, or anything having to do with your pricing.

- *Pros:*
  - Standards reduce the cost of doing business.
  - You can have an impact on creating and maintaining the standard if you are interested.

- *Cons:*
  - Once a company has invested the time, money and effort to code to a standard, once a new standard comes out it is almost impossible to get them to change. The only thing that I have seen that will make companies make the investment is government regulation. If a company is going to be out of compliance and possibly fined, then the work will get done.

- *Things to be aware of:*
  - Nobody will implement a standard in a standard way.
    * I know this sounds illogical but it is just the way things are. Although you will need to make custom changes for most of your customers you interface with, the time and effort to make those changes are negligible, especially when compared to having a different interface with each customer you do business with.
  - You will need to maintain multiple versions of the same standard.
    * Not all of your trading partners will move at the same speed when updating and maintaining their systems. Older customers that you have been integrated with for some time may be on one standard, but a new customer that is just building their interfaces will come up on the latest standard available.

- You may want to become a professional cake decorator.
  * Putting this in to see who is paying attention. If you decide to participate in a standards body, I just want to give you a word of caution. When you get a bunch of geeky/nerdy types who are passionate about their technology all in a room together, things can get out of hand. I witnessed a three-hour discussion/argument over the definition of the word "identifier". It was like being at the scene of an accident. I wanted to leave but I just couldn't stop myself from watching. Not to mention the holy war that was waged when defining the XML to be either "element centric" or "attribute centric". Technically it doesn't matter, but different people have very strong opinions both ways. Ultimately only one way can be selected and there can be a lot of hurt feelings.

Wherever you have influence in those first stages of setting up with a new trading partner, ensure a standard is agreed to. You will be helping your business to save money, time, and resources - and making your own job easier. Although no one implements a standard in a standard way, starting with one and making specific necessary changes is far better than the chaos of using no standards at all.

02

> Implementing a strategy for a secure file exchange, like implementing standards as far as possible, involves early agreement with your trading partner on the levels and type of security that are required by the task or by policy.

> CHAPTER TWO

Encryption and Security

Accepting that things can and do go wrong in the world of EDI is a big part of the job, but when it comes to security there is no excuse for not getting it right the first time. Or, in instances where you are inheriting a legacy system that should be more secure, make sure you develop and communicate a strategy to make it good as soon as possible.

File Transfer Protocol (FTP)

I mention FTP here simply because it will be something you will run into. I see no reason that it should ever be used in any type of business situation when there are other protocols that are available that are easier to use. The only way I would ever agree to transferring data using the FTP protocol is if it is required by your trading partner. Even then I would urge you to try and talk them out of it and use SFTP instead.

FTP was created back in the early 1970's before there was ever anything called a hacker. The deficiencies of the protocol should not be blamed on the people who created it. Just like the Y2K problem, people that were building systems back in the sixties and seventies weren't planning on how things would work, or look, forty years into the future.

22 | DATA HERDING

From a networking stand point FTP is bad because it requires you to open up a wide range of ports. The protocol will make the initial connection on port 21, but once the connection is authenticated, the client and server will agree on a higher port to send the actual data through. This can be any port above 6025. The more ports you open, the bigger your threat target is to an outside attacker. You will also need to determine ahead of time who will be allowed to determine the higher port to send the data over, the sender or the receiver. Usually, the receiver wants to reserve that right for themselves, so they can control which ports the need to open up. This is something you will need to sort out ahead of time.

- **Pros:**
  - It is ubiquitous, software is on almost every server by default.
  - It's easy to use.
- **Cons:**
  - There's no security at all. Data as well as credentials are transmitted in clear text.
  - You need to add your own security layer to it.
  - Even if you use PGP to encrypt the data, the credentials (username and password) are still sent in plain text.
  - If you are transferring data that is not regular ASCII (PDF files, Excel Spread Sheets, PGP encrypted data, etc.,) then you have to make sure to switch the transfer mode to binary, or the data will not be readable when it arrives at its destination.

- *Things to be aware of:*
    - It isn't secure
        * I want to mention this again. This will be raised as a security issue on an audit.
        * Username/Password and all data is sent in clear text over the public network between trading partners.
    - FTP uses port 21 to make the initial connection to a remote server. Once the connection is made the two servers will decide on a higher port to actually transmit the data. Port 21 is what is called the control port, and the other port is what is known as the data port. You have to make sure that any port that could be used by the FTP protocol is open.

SSH File Transfer Protocol (SFTP)

SFTP became available in the early 2000's. It was created to specifically overcome the security issues of FTP. The first computer virus released "into the wild" occurred in 1986. It wasn't even malicious, but things have gone downhill very quickly ever since.

There are a lot of negotiations that must occur between the server and client before files can be sent via SFTP. The server will have a preferred set of algorithms to use for security, but there must be at least one algorithm supported by both the sender and receiver in order for the communication channel to be established.

There are also different types of algorithms that need to be negotiated as well. One is for the types of keys to be used (either RSA or DSA). One is for the cipher to be used for encrypting the data (triple DES for example). One is for authenticating the messages sent back and forth, these are known as MAC or Message Authentication Code algorithms. And lastly the key exchange algorithm for establishing the keys to be used between the client and server.

These algorithms will need to be curated over time. Some will need to be disabled, and newer ones will need to be added as the security landscape changes. You have to maintain contact with your trading partners during your curating process to make sure that you all have a common set of algorithms available or your SFTP connections will fail.

I know this all sounds complicated, but it really isn't. Whatever SFTP software you are using will document how to do this (even the free ones). Usually, the curating process is nothing more than downloading the latest version of the software.

- *Pros:*
    - Its ubiquitous, software is on almost every server by default.
    - SFTP provides security of data while in flight.
    - It's easy to use.
    - The protocol can be used in conjunction with SSH keys which helps with the overhead of password maintenance.
- *Cons:*
    - It's slower than FTP due to the back-and-forth nature of the protocol.
- *Things to be aware of:*
    - Technology Advances
        * As new algorithms become available, and older ones become compromised, you will need to make sure you and your trading partners are able to maintain security.

- Trouble shooting
  * If you are having problems making an SFTP connection there are some handy parameters you can put on the command line to help troubleshoot issues.
    - sftp -v username@hostname
      - The -v means verbose and will give you information on the initial exchange between the two servers.
    - sftp -vv username@hostname
      - The -vv means very verbose and will give you more information on the initial exchange between the two servers.
    - sftp -vvv username@hostname
      - The -vvv means (you guessed it) very, very verbose and will give you even more information.
  * I would recommend that you use these commands, even if you aren't having any connection problems, so you will gain a better understanding of what is going on under the covers.
- SFTP uses port 22 to make the initial connection between servers. This is the only port used for the transmission. Port 22 is used for both control and data. This is why the protocol is slower than FTP.
- You will also hear SFTP referred to as Secure File Transfer Protocol.
- SSH stands for Secure Shell.
  * It allows for the strong authentication and encrypted data communications between two computers connecting over an open network (the internet).

Hypertext Transfer Protocol Secure (HTTPS)

If you have browsed the internet at all, then you should be familiar with HTTP / HTTPS. The difference between HTTP and HTTPS is the same as the difference between FTP and SFTP. HTTP is not secure, and should never be used in any type of business transaction, while HTTPS is secure and all data transfers are encrypted. HTTPS is usually used to manually send files, while the other protocols we have discussed are used to send files in an automated fashion, although either protocol can be used in either manner. Your trading partner, using their internet browser of choice, will log onto your server and upload files through the browser. Depending on how the user interface is implemented the trading partner could browse their local system to select a file to upload, or they could be allowed to simply drag and drop a file from their local machine to yours.

HTTP uses port 80 for traffic while HTTPS uses port 443. We will discuss white listing later in this chapter, but one advantage HTTPS could have over FTP/SFTP is that port 21/22 are generally white listed, while port 443 is not. This can make establishing the initial connection with your trading partner easier.

Applicability Statement 2 (AS2)

AS2, under the covers, is using HTTPS for its communication. All of the files are encrypted during transit, and no credentials are viewable from the outside when communications are taking place. AS2 allows the sender to request a Message Disposition Notification (MDN), also known as a receipt. The MDN is created and returned after the file has been successfully decrypted by the receiver. This provides the sender with "legal proof" that the file was successfully delivered without being altered in transit. When initially setting up AS2 communications; certificates used for encrypting, decrypting, and signing the data files are usually exchanged between the trading partners. The certificates are usually only good for a limited period of time, one or two years. Before the certificates expire, they will need to be updated, exchanged between trading partners, and installed on a coordinated basis so the communication channel does not stop working. I've generally encountered AS2 when exchanging financial transactions.

File Transfer Protocol Secure (FTPS)

FTPS is the same as FTP, but it allows for encryption of both the data and the credentials without the need for any third-party product (PGP). If you use port 21 to establish an FTPS connection, then you must initially send the command to encrypt the channel, if you fail to do this then the communication will be just plain FTP. This is what is known as explicit encryption, you must explicitly declare that you want to encrypt the communication channel. However, if you use port 990 the communication will be encrypted by default. This is what is known as implicit encryption, and is the preferred method for implementing FTPS. Just like FTP, FTPS uses one port for control (port 21 or 990) and another port to send the data (any port above 6025).

I can only think of one trading partner that has ever asked me to implement a file exchange using FTPS.

Note: Differences between FTP, FTPS, and SFTP. FTPS is the same protocol as FTP, but it adds a security layer on top of it. SFTP is a different protocol entirely. FTPS like FTP uses separate ports for control and data. So, if you were to use FTPS you would need to open up a range of ports to allow communication between the two servers. If you are using SFTP, however, then you only need to open up port 22.

SSH Keys - Secure Shell Keys

SSH keys can be used in conjunction with SFTP as an extra layer of security. It is a way to allow connections without requiring a password. You will still need to have a valid user-name for the server you are connecting to. The SFTP protocol will first check to see if there is a key available for the incoming connection. If there is a key then it will use it to authenticate and not prompt for a password. If there is no key then it will prompt for a password.

SSH keys are very similar to PGP keys. You will need to create a key pair (public and private) and give the public key to your trading partners that your sever will be connecting to. Likewise, if your trading partner wants to use a key to connect to your sever, then you will need to know how to install their key correctly.

- *Pros*
    - Will solve a lot of problems around having to manage passwords including:
        * Storing in property files in clear text which could be flagged in an audit, and is generally not a good practice.
        * Having to manage encrypting and decrypting credentials during the process of making a connection which is an unnecessary overhead that you will need to manage.
    - Key management is built into a lot of commercially available EDI solutions.

- You are not required, by technology, to have the key expire.
  * Company policy, or your trading partner may require an expiration be placed on keys.
- They are more secure than passwords.

- **Cons**
  - SSH keys are more complicated than simple user-name and password authentication.
  - You will be dependent on trading partners to install your public key correctly. You may be surprised at the lack of knowledge on how to do this.
  - People will get confused on who needs to install whose key.
    * The server initiating the connection will need to have its public key installed on the remote server.

- **Things to be aware of**
  - Technology advances
    * Integrators will need to stay abreast as new more secure hashing algorithms become available. If you are using an algorithm that has been compromised then you will need to generate new more secure keys and get them out to your trading partners.
    * Whatever algorithm you use to generate your key pair your trading partner will need to support the same algorithm. This is so the secure channel can be established and the encryption and decryption can take place on either end.

- If you want to use an algorithm not supported by a trading partner, getting them to implement it for your benefit could be problematic. If some customers support your preferred algorithm and some do not, then you will need to manage multiple keys. You will also need to be prepared for one of your trading partners to ask you to implement a stronger algorithm on their behalf.

* If you decide to have an expiration period on your key(s), then you will need to make sure to get the new key out to your trading partners before your current key expires. You may need to support both keys for a period of time.

Pretty Good Privacy (PGP)

In order to use PGP, you will first need to create a key pair. This is not difficult to do and will be documented in whatever PGP software you are using (even the free ones). As part of the process you will need to enter a pass phrase that you must remember. Once the process is complete you will have two keys. One is your public key and will probably have the suffix ".pub", and the other is your private key.

The two keys are mathematically linked together. Theoretically whatever is encrypted using the public key can only be decrypted using the private key. There have been several documented instances where people's personal electronic devices have been confiscated by governments, and they have not been able to access PGP encrypted files.

The public key is what you share with your trading partners, and it is the key they must use when they encrypt data before sending it to you. There are no restrictions on how you share your public key. The private key, however, is something that you need to maintain strict control over. It should be secured as well as the pass phrase used during the key generation process. The private key and pass phrase, in combination, are needed to decrypt files.

- **Pros**
    - PGP provides a security layer when data is in flight, as well as when it is at rest.
    - It's relatively easy to use
    - PGP capability is built into a lot of commercially available EDI solutions.
    - Free and good solutions are readily available.

- **Cons**
    - A lot of your external trading partners will be confused about the key exchange.
    - Managing keys becomes more difficult if there are multiple environments (development, integration, production) and there are different keys for each environment.
        * Your trading partners may use the wrong key for the environment, for example they will use the test key to encrypt and then send the data to your production environment, and vice versa.

- **Things to be aware of**
    - The public key is always used to encrypt.
        * Your trading partner must use your public key to encrypt the data before they send it to you.

- The private key is always used to decrypt.
    * You maintain control over your private key and the pass-phrase used to generate it. This must be kept secure.
- Internal testing is more difficult
    * If you are using PGP in your system, then you can't simply drop a file in your inbound location and run a test. You will need to make sure and encrypt the file first. I would not recommend skipping this part of the test because then it is not a valid test. Skipping this part has bitten me in the past.
- Archiving
    * I am going to harp a lot about archiving and how important it is. It is important to archive any file that you send to a customer. There is no reason you need to archive the encrypted version of the file, however. Once you use their public key to encrypt the data, then theoretically there is no possible way for you to read that file.
- Keep your private keys private, and in a secure place. You will also need to keep the pass phrase associated with each key secure. Keeping information secure, yet at the same time accessible, can be difficult.

PGP encryption has nothing to do with the protocol used to actually transfer a file from one system to the other. It is a completely separate and independent step. The encryption must be done before sending the file.

I would like to say that once you and your trading partner have the keys sorted out, then things will work from that point forward. It has been my experience, however, that is not always the case. I have had trading partners, seemingly at random, send data to my production server encrypted with the test key.

I personally do not see a problem using the same key for both test and production, but this is a policy decision that needs to be made at a management level.

I just want to give an example of what you may run into when using PGP encryption to exchange files with a trading partner. I spent the better part of two months in email exchanges with a person from a large bank explaining that they needed to send me a new PGP key in order to meet their security standards. I kept trying to get them to send me the account that was being used for me to send them encrypted data, and the type of data I was sending them (invoice file, reconciliation file, etc.). I just could not find where that was happening on my system. When it all got sorted out, it was actually encrypted data they were sending to me. When I pointed out that they would need a new key from me if they wanted to change that process, I never heard from them again.

Data in flight vs Data at rest

I mentioned previously about data in flight verses data at rest so I will illustrate what I mean by that. In the below diagrams I am showing server one, on the left, sending a data file to server two, on the right.

In the first example *(figure 1)*, I am depicting what that looks like using FTP. The data in flight looks exactly the same way the data looks on the sending server as well as the receiving server. I am also indicating that the username and password are being sent in clear text. The data is indicating a file containing the social security number of someone.

34 | DATA HERDING

It may not be unusual for you to transfer this type of data depending on what type of industry you are in. If you have a social security number then there is probably other personal data in the file as well (name, address, etc.). This is why it is so important not to use FTP in any type of file transmission. In this example the data is neither secure while in flight nor at rest.

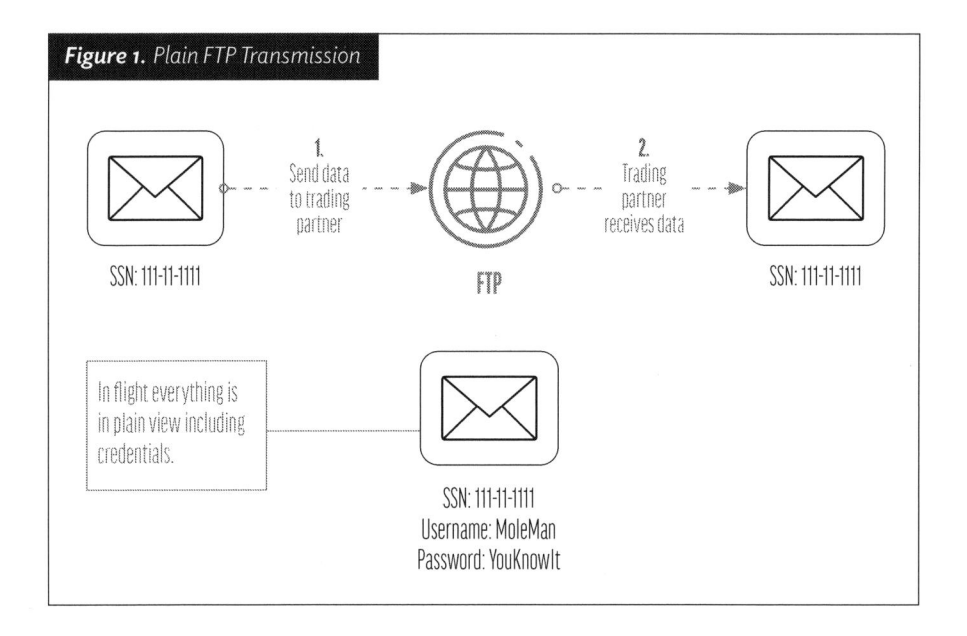

Figure 1. Plain FTP Transmission

```
   [✉]  --1.-->  (🌐)  ----->  [✉]
 SSN:111-11-1111  Send data   FTP   Trading   SSN:111-11-1111
                  to trading        partner
                  partner           receives data
                                    2.

 ┌─────────────────┐
 │ In flight       │         [✉]
 │ everything is   │
 │ in plain view   │     SSN: 111-11-1111
 │ including       │     Username: MoleMan
 │ credentials.    │     Password: YouKnowIt
 └─────────────────┘
```

In the second example *(figure 2)*, below, I am showing what it looks like using SFTP. While the data is in flight between the two systems the data is encrypted. As soon as the file comes to rest on the receiving server it is back in clear text, however. The username and password are also encrypted and not being sent in clear text. The effort in using SFTP is exactly the same as using FTP. There are no extra steps and the commands are identical. There is absolutely no reason why FTP should be used instead of SFTP. In this example the data is secure while in flight, but not at rest.

Figure 2. SFTP Transmission

1. Send data to trading partner
2. Trading partner receives data

SSN: 111-11-1111
SFTP
SSN: 111-11-1111

In flight everything is secure.

At rest everything is back in clear text.

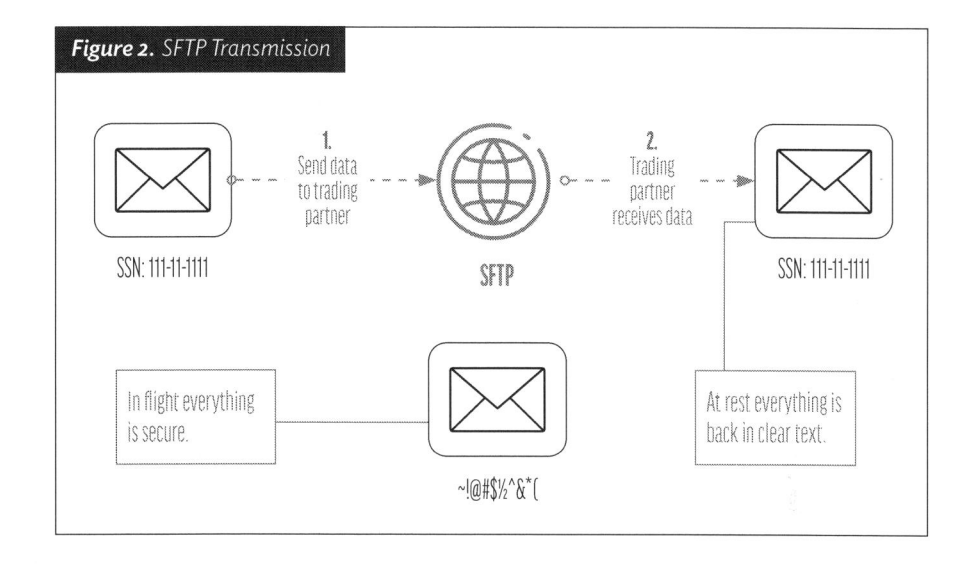

~!@#$½^&*(

In the third example *(figure 3)*, I am showing what it looks like using FTP plus PGP. Using PGP requires an extra step on both the sending side and the receiving side. The sending side must first use the specific public key for the trading partner they are sending the file to, and encrypt the file before sending it. The receiving side must use their private key to decrypt the file before they can process it. When the file arrives on the receiving server it is still encrypted. In this example the data is secure while both in flight and at rest. While using the FTP protocol the username and password are still being sent in clear text, however.

The receiving system should not decrypt the file until it is out of their demilitarized zone (DMZ) and in a more secure location on their network (I will discuss this in more detail later). Before sending PGP encrypted data using FTP, the sender of the data must make sure that the transfer mode is switched to binary before executing the put command. If they do not do this then the data will not be able to be decrypted on the receiving server.

Figure 3. FTP+PGP Transmission

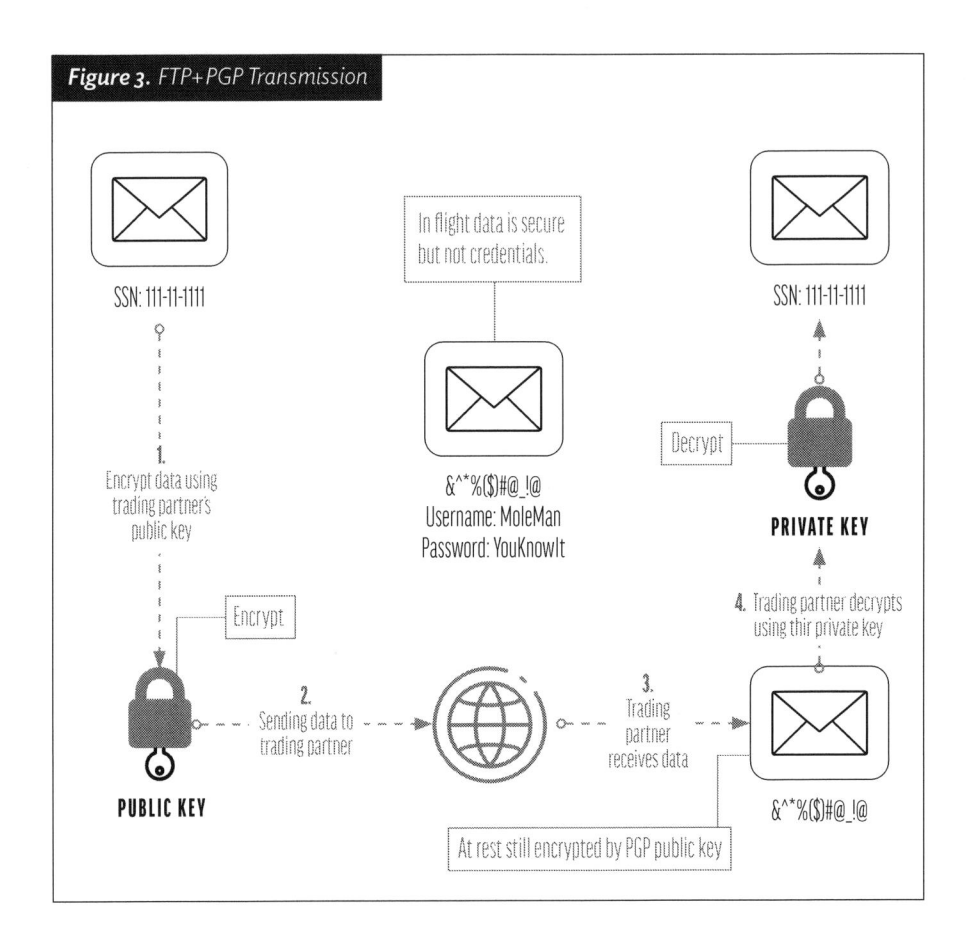

In the fourth example *(figure 4)*, I am showing what it looks like using PGP plus SFTP. It is the same as the one above it, however, the username and password are not being sent in clear text. While the data is in flight it is actually being encrypted a second time.

ENCRYPTION AND SECURITY | 37

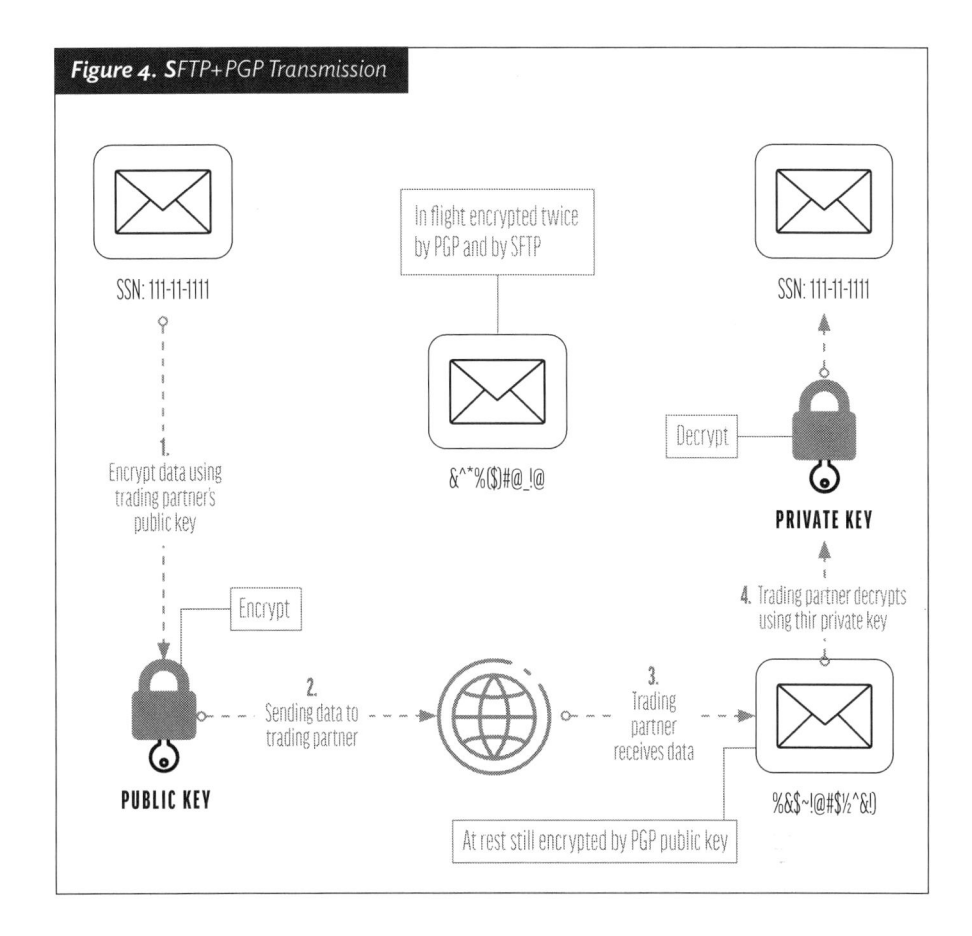

Figure 4. **S**FTP+PGP Transmission

I think it is obvious that the way to go is to use both SFTP and PGP together. This provides a very secure method for transmitting files.

If you are using PGP encryption with multiple trading partners then you will need to be able to know which key to use to encrypt data for which customer. I know this sounds obvious, but it is something to keep in the back of your mind when setting things up. You will need customer specific directories (or some other mechanism) to keep things straight.

Processing in the DMZ

The server or servers that are used to communicate with your external customers are going to logically be placed toward the exterior of your network. This makes them inherently less safe because there will be fewer security measures between the server and the public Internet. This is not a networking book, nor am I an authority on networking, so I will not get into details; but there should be at least one firewall between any server you are working with and the public internet *(firewall 1 in the diagram below, figure 5)*. There should also be another firewall (firewall 2 in the diagram below) between a server communicating with your trading partners, and the core network of your organization. The area in between these two firewalls is what is called the Demilitarized Zone (DMZ).

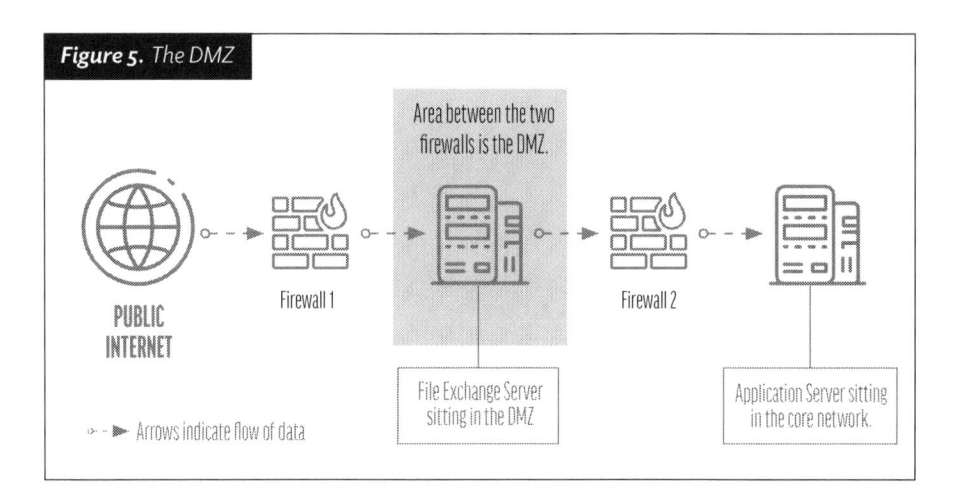

Figure 5. The DMZ

The diagram above, figure 5, illustrates what most networks look like. Servers that are communicating directly with external customers (web servers, file exchange servers, etc.) will probably reside in the DMZ area. There could be a third firewall creating what is known as a dual

DMZ network, but for the purposes of our discussions we will use the diagram above as our network layout.

In the text describing figure three above, I mention that data should not be decrypted until it is out of the DMZ and in a more secure location. *Figure 6* below illustrates what I mean by that.

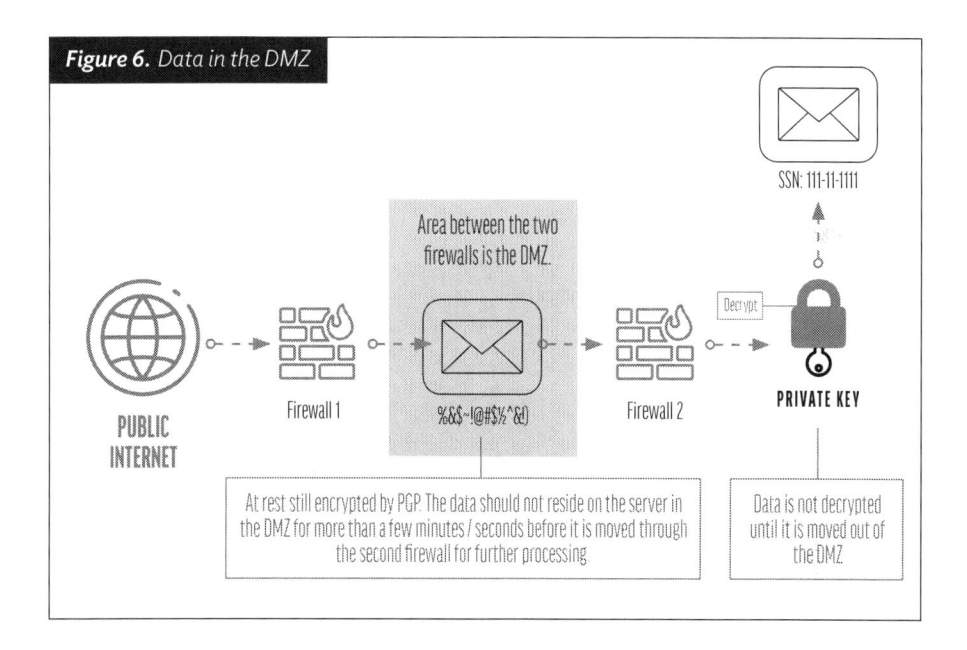

Figure 6. Data in the DMZ

[Diagram: Public Internet → Firewall 1 → DMZ (area between the two firewalls, containing encrypted data %&$~!@#$½^&()) → Firewall 2 → Decrypt → Private Key → SSN: 111-11-1111

At rest still encrypted by PGP. The data should not reside on the server in the DMZ for more than a few minutes / seconds before it is moved through the second firewall for further processing.

Data is not decrypted until it is moved out of the DMZ.]

How long the data sits in the DMZ is something that you can control on your own systems. You can't control what your external customers do, however. The data should not reside in the DMZ for more than a few seconds or minutes. The data should not be there for hours, and it certainly should not be there for days. This is why I recommend using PGP encryption when possible, because your trading partner could leave data in the DMZ forever! Generally, you will not have any knowledge of how your trading partner handles your data. As long as your data is encrypted, the chances of it being misused by a third party are decreased exponentially.

White Listing

Having a firewall between your file exchange server and the open internet provides the opportunity to use a White List. A white list adds another layer of protection between the public internet and your file exchange server. Only external servers that are specifically on the White List are allowed access to your server. A White List entry usually consists of the **From Address** (your external customers server), the **To Address** (your server that the external customer is connecting to) and the **Protocol** (FTP, SFTP, HTTPS, etc.). In order for a connection to be allowed all three things must match up.

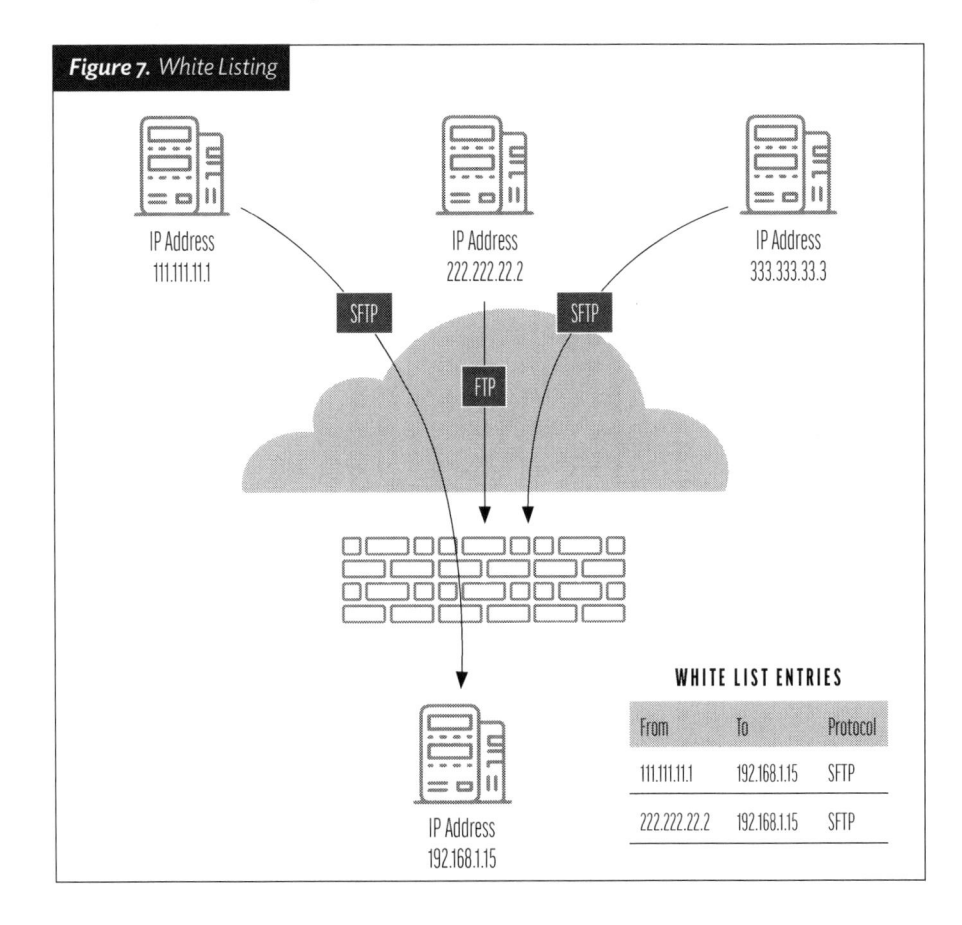

Figure 7. *White Listing*

IP Address
111.111.11.1

IP Address
222.222.22.2

IP Address
333.333.33.3

IP Address
192.168.1.15

WHITE LIST ENTRIES

From	To	Protocol
111.111.11.1	192.168.1.15	SFTP
222.222.22.2	192.168.1.15	SFTP

In our example above *(figure 7)*, a connection from the server with an IP address of 111.111.11.1 is allowed through the firewall because there is a valid entry in the White List for it. The connection from the server with an IP address of 222.222.22.2 is not allowed through because even though it is in our White List, it is not using the correct protocol. The connection is coming in using FTP, but our White List entry specifies that it must be SFTP. The connection from the server with an IP address of 333.333.33.3 is not allowed through because there is no entry in our White List for that server.

The decision to White List or not is a policy decision that should be made at the management level of your organization. It is entirely possible that you may white list traffic coming into some servers but not others. You would not want to restrict anyone from gaining access to your company's main web page for example, but you may want to White List access to a server that does nothing but provide file transfers between yourself and your external customers.

- *Pros:*
  - White listing provides another level of security to your organization.
- *Cons:*
  - It's an overhead that needs to be managed and planed for.
  - Your trading partner will change their IP address and not tell you about it. Then communications that have worked for years will all of a sudden stop. Since this is happening before your customer is actually getting to your sever, you will not have any indication of this until the customer reaches out to you letting you know they are having a problem.

- **Things you should know:**
  - You cannot test that the white list entry has been set-up correctly. If you are not coming from an IP address specifically on the list you should get an error. *There are ways to spoof an IP address but I would not recommend that you do this. Even if you have the permission of your organization it puts you in a gray area legally.*
  - If your Trading Partner decides that they are going to white list their outbound traffic (and a lot of them will) then Oh My Goodness the number of hours that you will waste trying to troubleshoot connection issues! I have generally found that the trading partner simply has not set up their networking properly. When you are troubleshooting these types of errors you will need to schedule a conference call that includes at least someone from the business unit of your trading partner, someone from their networking team, someone from your internal networking team, and yourself. Your customer's business unit will need to initiate a transaction from their server to yours. Their networking person will need to follow the traffic from their internal network out to the internet. And then your networking person will need to see that it makes it to your specified server. If the stars are all aligned you can usually figure out what is going on and resolve whatever the issue is. It has been my experience, however, that it takes at least a couple of tries before you get all of the right people, at the right place, looking at the right thing, all at the same time.

Implementing a strategy for a secure file exchange, like implementing standards as far as possible, involves early agreement with your trading partner on the levels and type of security that are required by the task or by policy. The challenges I've lived through described in this chapter, mostly involving keys, can be avoided by clear communication with trading partners and remembering that your way of ensuring encryption and security, may be different than what they are used to.

03

> The best way to figure out what went wrong, when, how, and why is to archive. Archive everything you receive from a trading partner, and everything you send to them.

> CHAPTER THREE

Interfacing to the Customer

Like we covered in previous chapters, early and clear communication is so important when setting up with a new customer and in managing existing relationships. Some of the key things you need to be talking about are your directory structures, and who pushes and who pulls the data. But as you probably know, EDI is a tricky beast and despite your best intentions and plans, sometimes things change or they go wrong. The best way to figure out what went wrong, when, how, and why is to archive. Archive everything you receive from a trading partner, and everything you send to them.

Directory Structure

When you are setting up a new connection with a trading partner there are two different approaches you can take. We will simply call them "Different Directory for each File Type" and "One Inbound Directory".

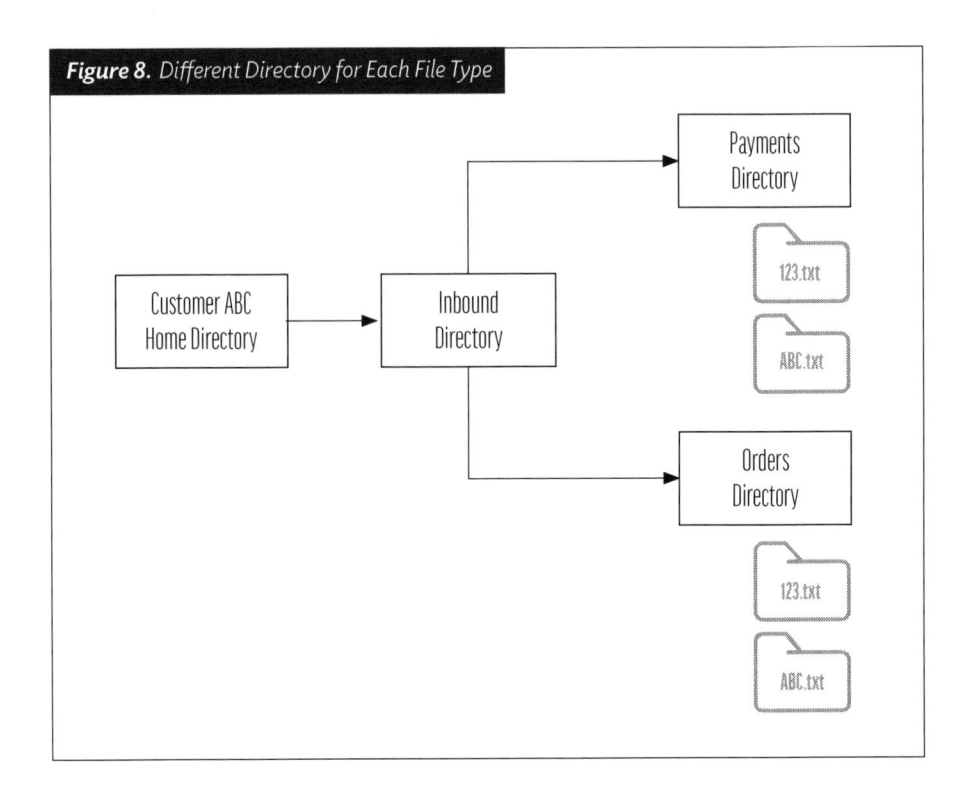

Figure 8. *Different Directory for Each File Type*

What I am trying to illustrate in the above diagram *(figure 8)*, is that if we use the model of having a different directory for each file type, then it really doesn't matter what the files are named. Everything that is in the Payments directory we know should be a payment file, and everything that is in the Orders directory we know should be an order file.

Figure 9. *One Inbound Directory*

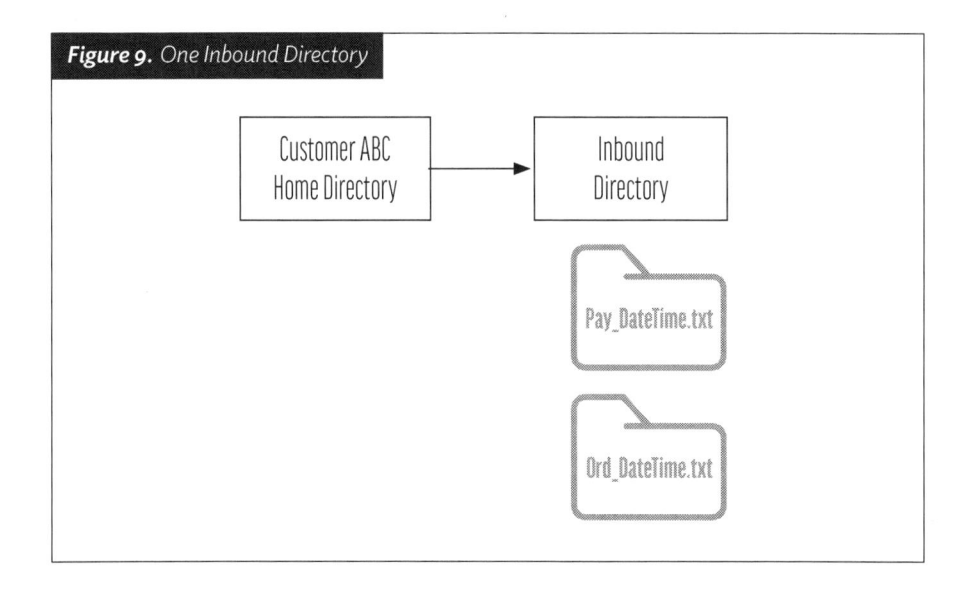

[Customer ABC Home Directory → Inbound Directory containing Pay_DateTime.txt and Ord_DateTime.txt]

If we go with the other model, however, then naming conventions are very very important. The naming convention must be agreed upon between you and your trading partner and they must be adhered to stringently. You can only discern what is a payment file or what is an order file by the name of the file itself. I generally try to have some demarcation in the file name so it is easy to parse out what type of file it is. I have an underscore in the above example *(figure 9)*, but you could use periods, dashes, or whatever you can agree to with your trading partner. I also like to have the file type at the very beginning of the name so it is easier to parse out.

- *Pros*
    - I think the first design, different directories for each file type, is a better implementation because there is less complexity. You don't need to parse the file name in order to know what action to take.

- ***Things to be aware of***
  - You can't try to bulldog your customer to meet your needs. I generally ask the customer if they have a preference one way or the other. If they have no opinion then I will try to guide them to use different directories for different file types.
  - You cannot come up with your own model and standardize on it. Different customers will have strong opinions on how to implement and you need to be accommodating.
  - It really doesn't matter which way you decide to go, because your trading partner is going to mess things up.
    * They will put payment files in the order directory and vice versa.
    * They will name files wrong.

You will need to have the same discussion for outbound files. It may not be the same. Your trading partner may want to place all of the files they are sending to you in one inbound directory, but they may want things in the outbound directory broken out by file type. They may want to push all of their files to your server into one inbound directory; but instead of retrieving the files from your server they may want you to push the files to them into separate directories by file type. I'm not going to diagram out all of the different scenarios but I think you get the picture.

Who pushes and who pulls

As mentioned above you will need to work out with your trading partner who will do the connecting and transmitting of files. Your trading partner can make the connection to your server and push files to you, and pull files from your server to theirs. I am illustrating that scenario below *(figure 10)*.

Figure 10. *Trading Partner Pushing and Pulling Files*

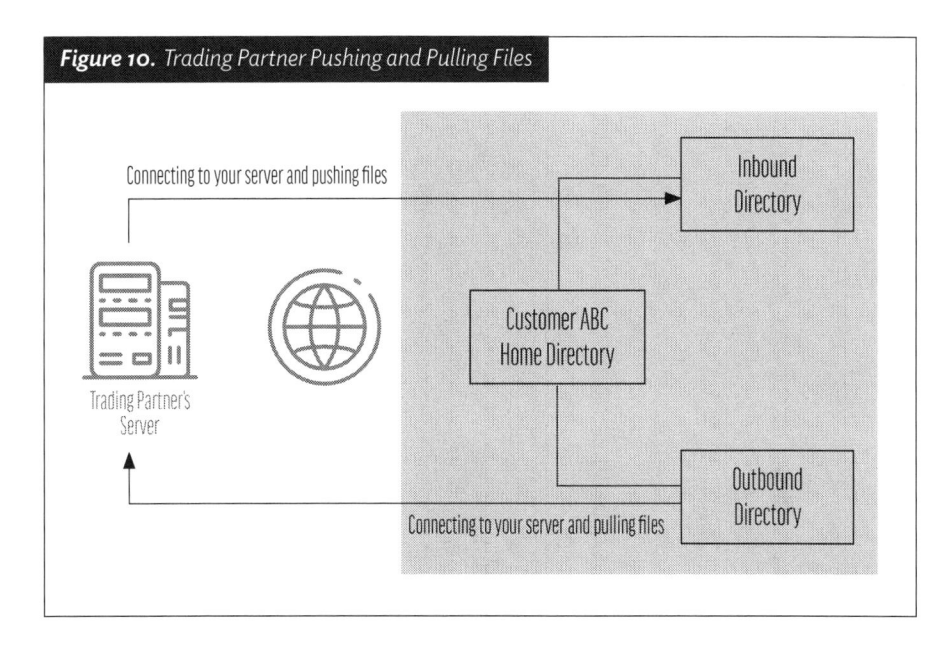

Or you can connect to your trading partners server and push files to them, and pull files from their server to yours. I'm illustrating that scenario below *(figure 11)*.

Figure 11. *Your Server Pushing and Pulling Files*

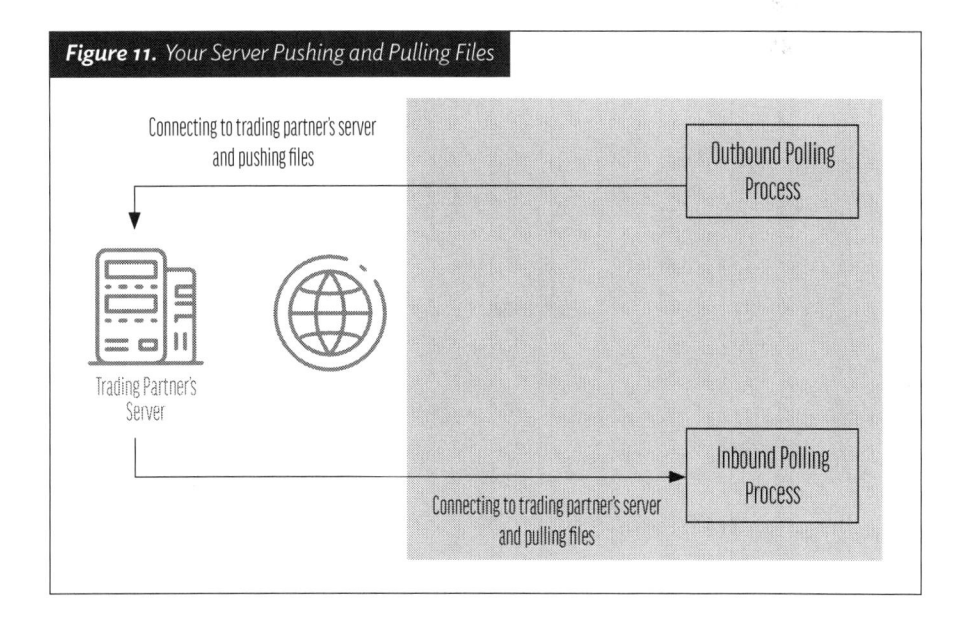

There is no technical reason why these two methods could not be combined. Your trading partner could connect to your server to push files to you, and you could connect to their server and push files to them. I'm not sure there is any right or wrong answer on how to do this, it is just one of the things you will need to work out with your trading partner at the very beginning.

- **Things to be aware of:**
  - I don't believe there is any right or wrong answer on how to transmit files.
  - Your trading partner may require that your server be white listed if you are connecting to them.
  - Your organization may require that the trading partners server be white listed if they are connecting to you.
  - If your server is going to be unavailable due to maintenance, or whatever reason, you may want to inform all of your trading partners about the downtime.
    * Having contact information handy for all trading partners will probably be problematic.
      - If your contact information is for individuals it will be out of date as soon as you have it.
      - You should get a distribution list from your trading partners for contact purposes instead of individual email accounts.
    * Even if you inform your trading partners about your down time, some will still transmit files during your outage and then want to know why they got errors.

Scheduled Inbound Poller

If the trading partner has normally scheduled down time (weekends for example) you would not want to be attempting connection attempts during that time and generating unnecessary errors. Your poller should mimic the uptime schedule of your trading partner.

Scheduled Outbound Poller

You should only make the connection to your trading partner if you have files to actually send. This is machine to machine communication so there is no reason to have the credentials expire. You don't want a maintenance nightmare. You could use SSH keys and then there would be no need for a password.

Archive Archive Archive

Once you place yourself in the middle of two systems, which is what EDI is all about, the finger pointing will start. Invariably things will go wrong and just as invariably you will get blamed for things that are not your fault. The only way to help troubleshoot, and prove your innocence, is to have your archives.

It is very important that you archive and that you archive every step of the way. You want to see what comes into a step, and what goes out of a step. In some use-cases it will just be where you pick up the file from one place and move it to another. In other use-cases where you do a data transformation, for example, you need to have both the input and the output. If you have a business process where there are many steps strung together you want to make sure you have the data flowing into and out of every step.

The archives can simple be flat files that are stored somewhere, or objects in a database.

You need to have what comes in from the customer, in the exact format as it comes from the customer. This could be important if there are ever legal issues around what was actually sent and received between different companies. I mentioned earlier that there is no need to archive the encrypted file that you send to a customer. You want to archive the encrypted file that you receive from the customer, however. You should always be able to decrypt the file. If you have a policy that you change keys every so often, or you change keys due to security concerns, you want to make sure you keep the old keys in case you need to decrypt a file from the past. You should have the archive of the decrypted file, but just in case there is a dispute and someone says well you must have decrypted it wrong (just saying) having the original file in its original state will be helpful.

One of the most important things to consider around archiving is how long you plan to keep the archived files. Once again this is dependent upon your use case (and maybe legal requirements). I generally keep things in a "short term" archive location for thirty days, and a "long term" location for one year. All data files should be backed up daily, so if you need to access files after a year's time then you would need to work with your system admins to recover the file(s) from the backup media. You have to do your best at estimating how much storage space you will need and making sure it is available.

When new systems are brought on line, or changes are made to existing systems, you will be referring to these archives quite frequently. As systems mature and get some age on them the archives will generally be used less and less.

One thing you will never get away from, however, is a problem occurring in some other process that your system is feeding, and the request to re-drop or re-send a particular file.

"We need you to re-drop the billing file that came in from customer ABC at 9:30 PM last Thursday". This is a legitimate request and you will need to be able to locate that file and re-process it in a timely manner.

Another thing that you need to consider is the audience for your archives and the access. If the archives are simply flat files out on disk somewhere, and someone in the business unit needs access to them, chances are you are going to have to manually locate the file and send it to them. If the archives are in a database, with a nice user interface allowing for searching, then the business unit can self-serve (or at least your job of getting the file to them is much simpler).

One solution is simple, and one is not. Like most things in life, it comes down to time, money, and effort.

If someone in the business unit asks to see the "raw data" and the data is in an X12 format, it is probably going to be meaningless to them. This is just one more thing to keep in the back of your mind.

And so now data has been exchanged. Hopefully it adheres to a standard, it was exchanged securely, and it followed all naming conventions (or whatever agreements) that you and your trading partner came up with. You should also have an archived version of the data - just in case. In the next part I will cover processing and all of the decisions and steps that may involve.

04

> Things can and will go amiss sometimes. As long as we have sufficient monitoring in place, we will know about it, and be able to resolve the issue (for the most part), before anyone else even realizes anything has happened.

> CHAPTER FOUR

Processing

All the different ways that incoming data can be processed are far too numerous for me to cover in detail here. The main thing to remember is that there isn't always a right or wrong way to process exchanged data. The most important thing to do with processing, though, is to plan a strategic design choice at the outset of the project. And stick to it, consistently.

What to do with newly received files

In the figure 12, below I am showing some of the things you may need to do with a file once you receive it. The further right you go in the diagram the closer you should be to handing the file off to another system, and the more you are opening yourself up to trouble.

Below I explain each of the first steps: move to a specific location, parse a file, send to a non-EDI service and send to an EDI service.

56 | DATA HERDING

Figure 12. *Processing a Received File*

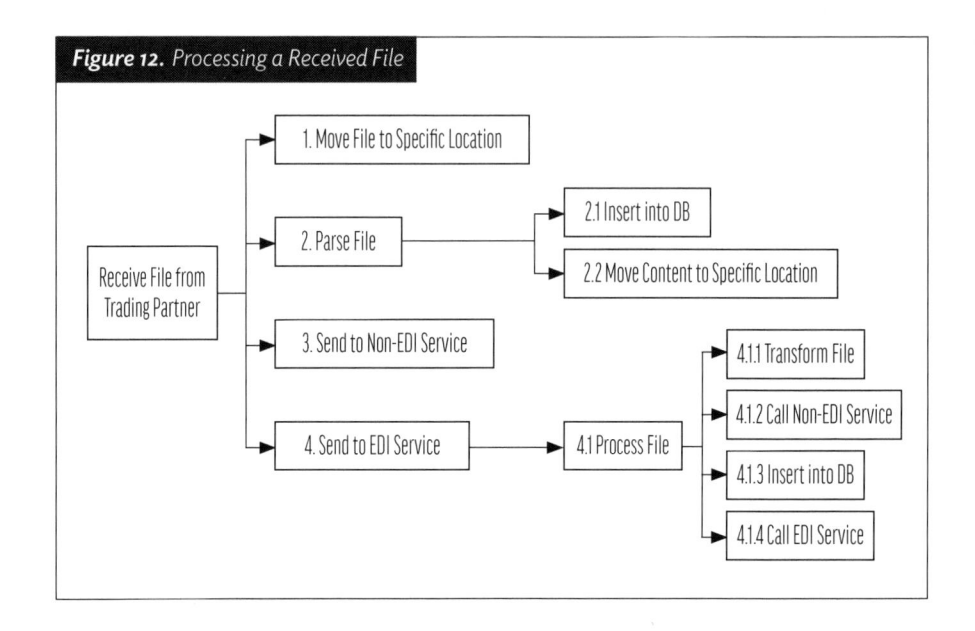

1. **Move to specific location**

   The first thing on our diagram is simply taking the file received and moving it to some location. From there it will be consumed by another system and your job is done.

- ***Things to consider:***
  - Archive the file you received from the customer.
    * I'm not going to call this out in all of the situations we consider, but this needs to happen every single time.
  - Make sure the file gets moved from its inbound location to the place you need to move it.
  - Once the file has been successfully moved make sure it is no longer in the inbound location.

* You don't want to process the same file over and over
* I'm not going to point this out in all of the situations we consider, but this needs to happen every single time.
- *What can go wrong:*
  - You get a file that you don't know how to process.
    * The naming convention is not what was agreed upon.
      - In the discussion we had above about the directory structure; if we are using the "one inbound directory" example then we are expecting files prefixed with PAY or ORD. Suppose we got a file prefixed with BIL. Our inbound polling process would not recognize this, and the file would just sit there in the Inbound directory forever.
  - You cannot move the file to the location
    * You don't have permission
    * The location is unavailable
      - If it is a mounted file system then the mount has gone away.
    * The file system where you are attempting to place the file has ran out of disk space.
    * At least fifty other things that I can't think of.

2. **Parse File**

It is not uncommon for the EDI space to have the responsibility of parsing, or transforming, a file that comes from a customer into the format that internal systems need to consume. Once this is done there can be a myriad of things you need to do with the transformed data. I am just showing two possibilities in figure 12.

- ***Things to consider:***
    - Archive the file you received from the customer.
        * If the file comes in encrypted then I would archive both the encrypted and unencrypted version.
    - Archive the parsed version of the file.

- ***What can go wrong:***
    - The file isn't in the format you are expecting so the parsing fails.

2.1 Insert into Database

- ***Things to consider:***
    - Should you be doing this at all or should this be some non-EDI system.

- ***What can go wrong:***
    - Database is unavailable
    - Data is parsed successfully but when you try to insert into the database you get a data mis-match error.
        * For example, an order number which should be numeric is actually alpha-numeric.
            - Should your parsing process catch this error?
                - Is it okay to just correct the data and reprocess the file?

- Are there legal implications?
  - Who contacts the customer about correcting their data and resending the file?

2.2 Placed parsed contents to specific location

Everything to consider and everything that can go wrong are captured above. But now the question that you need to plan for is if the data is wrong (alpha numeric order number) whose problem is that? Is it your problem to try and resolve, or is it the system that you have handed the file off to? Who contacts the customer? Who corrects the data and re-drops? This is a boundary where roles and responsibilities need to be defined and people held accountable.

3. Send to non-EDI service

In this scenario we are placing a service call and passing the contents of the file to a service. The service we are calling is not in our area of responsibility.

- **Things to consider:**
  - If the service hands back any kind of response make sure you archive it.

- **What can go wrong:**
  - The service is unavailable.
  - All of the data issues and questions in the other scenarios above.

4. **Send to EDI service**

    In this scenario we are placing a service call and passing the contents of the file to a service. Here, however, it is a service that is within our area of responsibility. We own the process that is consuming the file. It could be a third-party product or it could be a process that we have built ourselves. What I am trying to illustrate is that whatever our service is doing, we have to keep track of it every step of the way.

- ***Things to consider:***
    - We need to archive the input and the output of every single step.
    - If a step encounters an error, we need to send a notification with enough information that we know what the error is and where it happened.

- ***What can go wrong:***
    - Everything!

    I am also showing the possibility of our EDI service calling another EDI service (4.1.4). If you are doing this then I believe you are really getting off the reservation. There has to be a point where your responsibility ends and another business unit takes over.

    If all we are doing with a file when we receive it is invoking another EDI service, then this could potentially be a service that we expose externally and have the trading partner call directly. I just want to point out this possibility, it is not something I'm going to get into a whole lot in this book. *Maybe the next one.*

    I know I have talked a lot in this section about things that can and will go wrong. In the next sections I will go over how to deal with these situations when things do take a turn toward chaos.

Polling Options

In the sequence diagram below *(figure 13)*, I want to point out two options that you have when a process encounters an error.

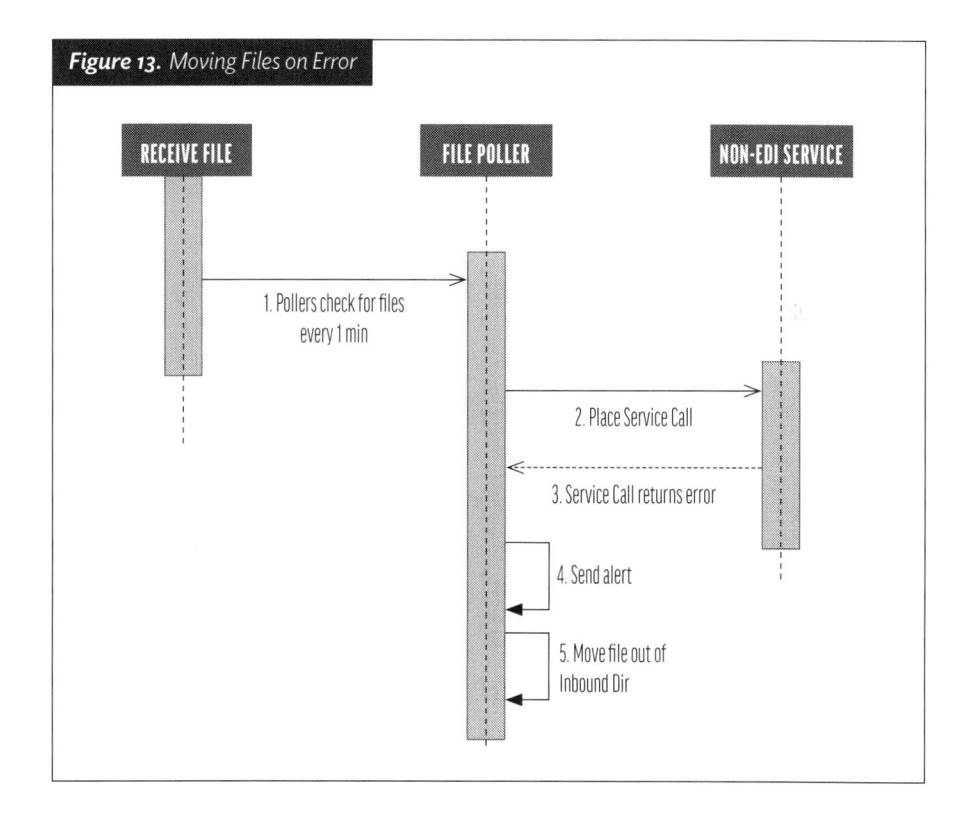

Figure 13. *Moving Files on Error*

1. Pollers check for files every 1 min
2. Place Service Call
3. Service Call returns error
4. Send alert
5. Move file out of Inbound Dir

Figure 13 is depicting a scenario where we are placing a service call to a non-EDI service, and it is encountering a problem and handing us back an error message. *If this were one of our services it would not return an error because it would just work.* Our polling process must do step 4, send an alert. For our purposes we are going to assume that all of our alerts are email messages. Step 5, however, can be an optional step.

We can decide to leave the files in place, or move the files out of our inbound directory. I have already mentioned that once we have successfully processed a file, we must move it out of the inbound directory in order to avoid the problem of processing the same file multiple times. But if we get an error while processing the file, we can either leave it in place, continuing to process the same file over until success, or move it out of the inbound directory to process later. If we decide that we are going to move the file(s) out of our inbound directory, we can either move them to an error location or the normal archive location. The alert that we send should contain the file name and enough information that we know exactly what the error was and where it was encountered. We need this information so we will know what file(s) we need to move back into the inbound directory after the problem has been resolved.

Moving the file(s)

- *Pros:*
    - You will not be flooded with emails.
        * If you are processing files every minute, and it takes two hours to resolve the problem, you are going to get 120 emails if you leave the files in the inbound directory.
        * If you have 10 files, all failing with the same service call, you will get 1,200 emails if you leave the files in the inbound directory.
- *Cons:*
    - You will not be flooded with emails if you move the files out of the inbound directory.
        * Some people like the idea of having the system complain about an error until it is resolved. This brings people's attention to the issue.

- Once the problem is resolved, someone will need to move the unprocessed files from the location they were moved to, back to the inbound directory.
  * If there are a lot of files and you have moved them to the archive directory you can usually do this by moving all files received after a certain time (the time you got the first email indicating there was an error).
  * If you have moved the file(s) to an error location then you would simply move all of the files in that location back to the inbound directory.
- If you simply leave the file(s) in the inbound directory, then once the problem is resolved, nobody has to do anything for all of the files to be processed as they normally would.

- ***Things to be aware of:***
  - If you leave the files in the inbound directory and something goes bad over a weekend, and people are not checking things until Monday morning, you can have a whole lot of emails when you get in.
  - If you decide to leave the files in the inbound directory and you know it will be a while before the problem can get resolved, you can always go and move the files out of the inbound directory manually until such time as the problem is fixed.
    * Files can continue to come into the inbound directory from your trading partners and you will need to keep moving them out.

There isn't a right or wrong answer here. I just want to make you aware that this is a design choice that you need to make. Whatever you decide, you need to be consistent with all of your processes.

Sending Notifications

In the sequence diagram below *(figure 14)*, I want to point out two options that you have when a process finishes successfully.

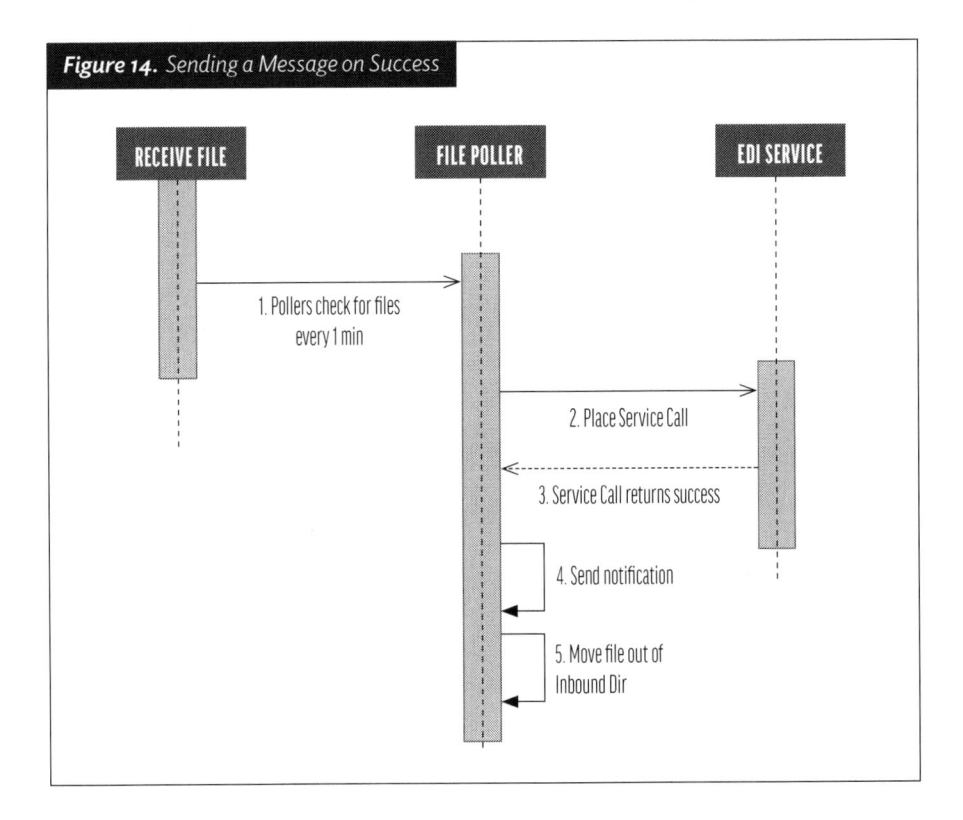

Figure 14. *Sending a Message on Success*

- RECEIVE FILE
- FILE POLLER
- EDI SERVICE

1. Pollers check for files every 1 min
2. Place Service Call
3. Service Call returns success
4. Send notification
5. Move file out of Inbound Dir

Figure 14 is depicting a scenario where we are placing a service call to an EDI service, and everything works as expected. *This is one of our services and it just works.* Now our polling process must do step 5, move the file so we are not continually processing the same file over and over.

Now step 4 is an option that we can choose to do or not do. Some people only want to send an email when there is an error. No need to bother people if everything is working as expected. Others, however, want to know whenever a file has been processed with or without error.

As above there isn't a right or wrong answer here either. Make a strategic design choice and stick to it consistently for all of your processes.

Scheduling

If you are feeding data to different back-end systems there are a couple of scenarios you may need to deal with. If all systems you are feeding are on the same schedule, then you can do everything in real time or "near time". I am diagramming what this may look like below (figure 15).

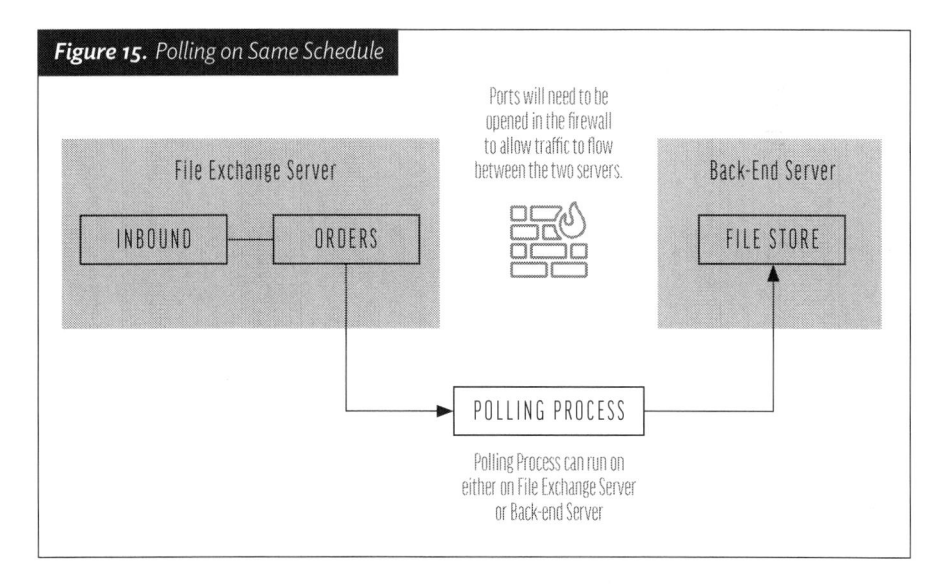

Figure 15. Polling on Same Schedule

66 | DATA HERDING

ment where systems are up and running twenty-four hours a day, then your polling process can be running all of the time. If the back-end system goes down between the hours of 12:00 AM and 1:00 AM you can shut down your polling process between the same hours. I have seen multiple situations where systems are down between 12:00 AM and 1:00 AM Monday through Saturday, but are down 12:00 AM to 4:00 AM on Sundays. You just need to mimic whatever schedule the back-end system follows.

Another situation you may have is that you are feeding data to different back-end systems that are on different schedules. If this is the case then you would probably be better served to move your files to a holding location, and then having separate polling processes move the files to the appropriate back-end system.

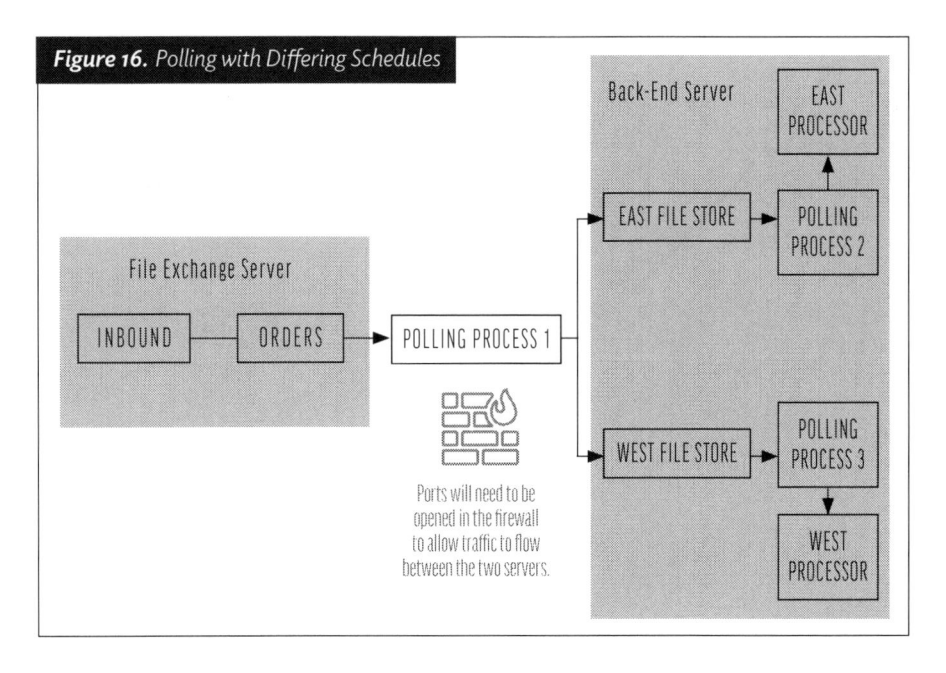

Figure 16. Polling with Differing Schedules

In the *figure 16* above, I am showing how something like this may appear. There would need to be a way to discern which files are for the East Coast and which ones are for the West Coast. This could be done either by file naming convention or having separate directories for each. Either way, once the files are in the "holding location" you can independently move them to the different back-end system, matching whatever schedule the system you are feeding follows. In our example above both back end systems may be available between 1:00 AM and 11:59 PM, but one is on East Coast time and the other is on West Coast time. By having two separate file stores and polling processes you can deal with this situation easily.

Generally speaking, whenever you are feeding another system, you are going to want the feed to that system to be isolated as illustrated above. The reasons for this are listed below:

o Different operating schedule as in our example.
o System goes down for maintenance
  * Simply stop the polling process from feeding it (either Polling Process 2 or Polling Process 3 in our example above).
o System goes down unexpectedly
  * Simply stop the polling process from feeding it. Depending on where the failure occurs, it could be any of the polling processes in our example above.
    • This will stop the emails from coming indicating there is an error with the back end system.
    • This will start the emails coming indicating that files are not being moved out of the inbound location.
    • *We will talk about monitoring and sending email alerts in the following chapters.*

If the feed is not isolated, and you have to stop the polling process due to one of the back end systems having a failure, then you are going to stop processing files in other systems that are up and available. This is not a desired outcome.

The server that is receiving files from your trading partners should generally be available twenty-four hours a day and seven days a week. The processes that are moving files around do not necessarily need to be running twenty-four by seven, but the server itself should be up and able to receive files.

Poor Mans Test System

I strongly encourage you to have a test system for every environment that your place of business supports. It is not uncommon to have environments for development, integration, user acceptance test (UAT), and production. Most of the other business units will have resources (money) that allow them to have separate machines for each environment. For whatever reasons, however, the EDI group seems to always be told to make do with what we have. We are not seen as important enough, or what we do is so simple, that we cannot justify having extra hardware. I urge you to fight the good fight to get what you need, but if it is just not something that is going to happen then you will need to create a directory structure like the one below *(figure 17)*.

Figure 17. Poor Man's Test System

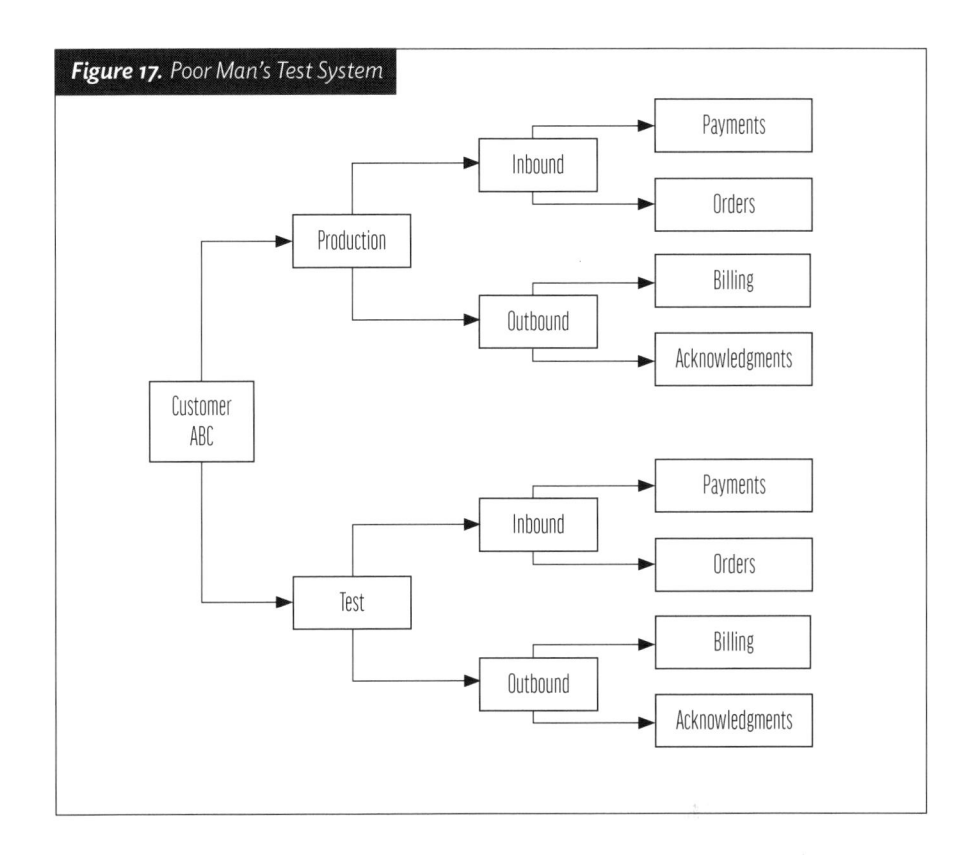

Your trading partners will be connecting to the same machine for both test and production but there will be separate, yet identical, directory structures for each environment. The demarcation between the different environments is at the highest level. There could potentially be other environments set up on the server, development and integration for instance. But there should be only one test environment that you use with your external trading partners. They will have enough issues just keeping test and production straight, no need to add to the confusion by asking them to integrate with multiple test systems.

You could also have different accounts for each customer. Account CustomerABC_PROD and account CustomerABC_TEST, for example.

I'm not sure one way is necessarily better than the other, they are both bad. The best way is to have a completely separate isolated system for each environment, but if that is not possible implement either a directory or account system.

In this section I have talked about processing files in the EDI space. I have also talked a lot about things going wrong. Things can and will go amiss sometimes. As long as we have sufficient monitoring in place, we will know about it, and be able to resolve the issue (for the most part), before anyone else even realizes anything has happened.

05

> If we have a monitor process that has to be modified every time we add a new customer, our monitor is going to break down. Trust me, this is one of those maintenance things that always gets overlooked even though we have the best of intentions.

> CHAPTER FIVE

Monitoring

Making sure you have sufficient monitoring and alerting in place; is the difference between having the system work for you, and you working for the system.

Directories

Figure 18 below is showing our file exchange server sitting in the DMZ. It is also showing our application server sitting behind our second firewall. The polling processes are shown moving files between the two servers.. The polling processes could be running on either server (it really doesn't matter). Ports (or holes) will need to opened up in the firewall to allow the traffic to flow between the two servers.

74 | DATA HERDING

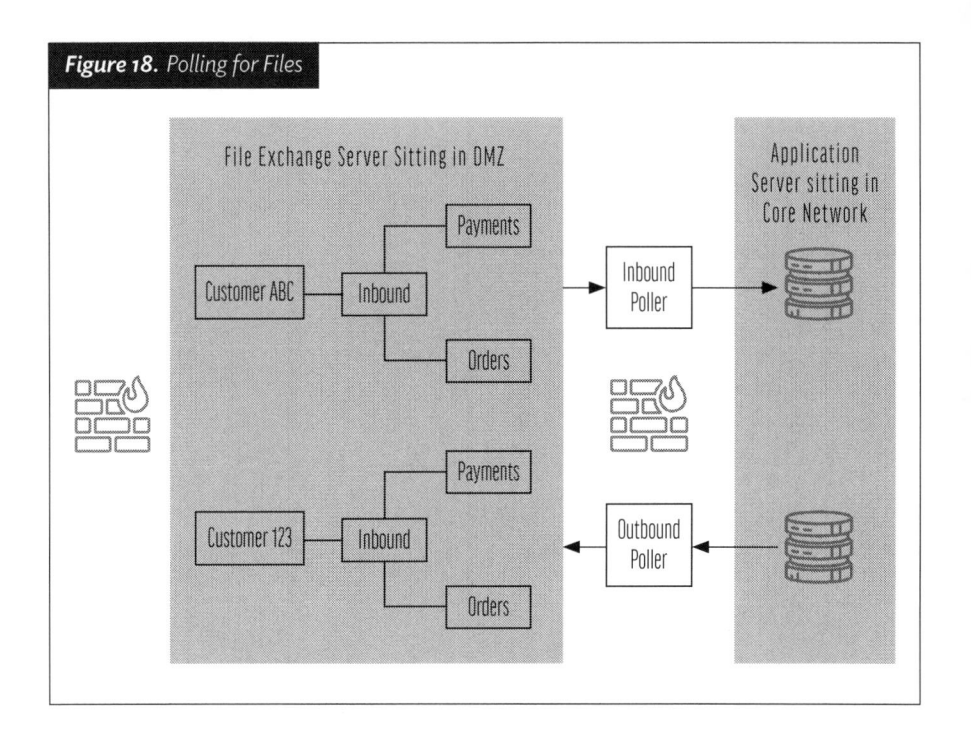

Figure 18. Polling for Files

I don't want to prescribe what your directory structure should look like on your file exchange server, but I do want to insist that you have a consistent naming convention and that it is adhered to. There needs to be separate accounts for each customer. Nobody should have access to anyone elses data other than their own. There should be a way to indicate the flow of data between you and your trading partners. In the above example *(figure 18)*, I am using Inbound and Outbound. The direction indicated should be relative to the server on which the directory is sitting (not to the external server). *This is a suggestion, and nothing written in stone, but it just makes everyone's life easier if we can just all agree on something.*

The main thing you want to monitor are the subdirectories under the Inbound directory. We will talk about the outbound later. Generally speaking, you are going to have your poller set up on a schedule to poll the Inbound/Payments directory (let's say every 5 minutes). So, if a file sits in that directory for more than thirty minutes, then you know there is a problem and you need to send an alert. Having an issue with your system is okay, nothing is perfect, but you need to know about it and react to it before either your internal business unit or your trading partner knows about it.

Below *(figure 19)*, is our same directory structure, but illustrating our inbound monitor process.

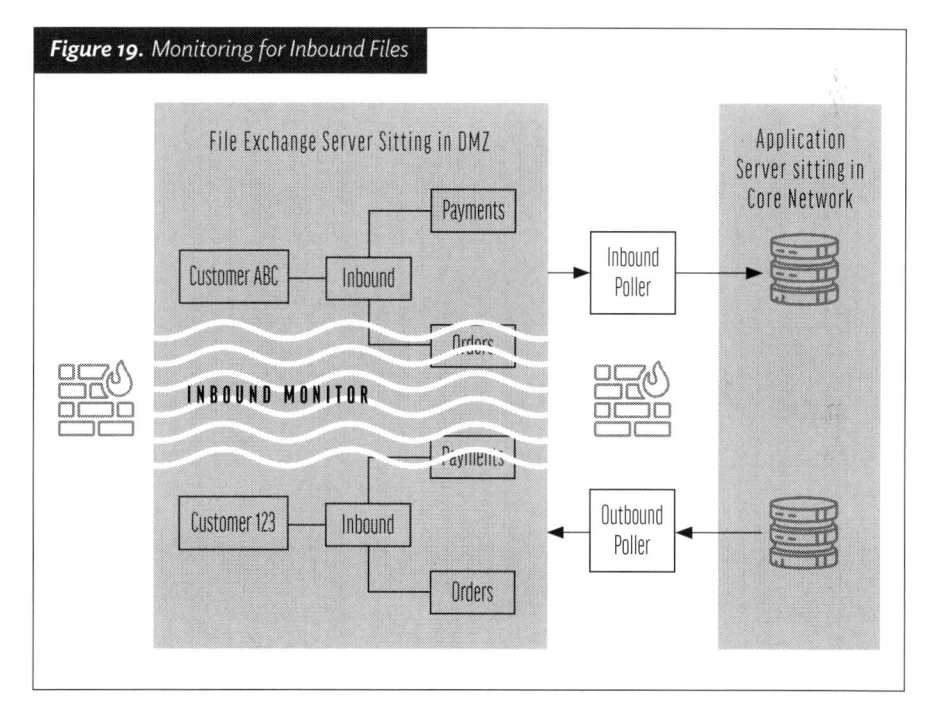

Figure 19. Monitoring for Inbound Files

Our inbound polling process is firing every five minutes. It is searching for inbound files on our file exchange server and moving them through the firewall back to our application server for processing. There is another polling process searching on our application server for files we need to place on our file exchange server for our customers to come pick-up. In the diagram above *(figure 19)*, I am showing two separate processes for the inbound and outbound polling, but it could be a single process, or it could be different processes for different file types, or some other configuration. Whatever the use case is, it just needs to cover all scenarios for your business.

We also have a monitor process (shown as a wave) that is checking our inbound directories every thirty minutes. It is searching for files that are older than thirty minutes. If it finds one then it needs to send an alert so someone will know to check why the file isn't being moved. Some of the common reasons files may be stacking up in our inbound area are:

- Our polling process is down.
- The file names are not matching our naming convention so the poller is ignoring them.
- Something has happened to the permission settings, resulting in our poller no longer being able to read/delete files

I want you to notice that the monitor process is starting at the root directory of our customers, and not one of the sub-directories. This is very important. If we have a monitor process that has to be modified every time we add a new customer, our monitor is going to break down. Trust me, this is one of those maintenance things that always gets overlooked even though we have the best of intentions. You need to have a monitor that is going to recursively go down a directory structure looking for files that meet your certain criteria. Whenever we add a new customer (a new directory to our structure) it will get monitored automatically without us having to do anything. This is why I stressed earlier about having a consistent naming convention for your directories.

The monitor process will start at the root directory where all of our "Customer" directories are located. It will start from that point, looking for all directories with a name of Inbound. Once it finds one then it would recursively search all directories underneath it for files that are older than thirty minutes. If there were sub-directories under Payments, then the monitor process would need to recognize that and search for files under that directory that are older than thirty minutes. The monitor process should be able to discern what is a directory and what is a file and "flow" down the directory structure searching for files that meet our criteria.

You will notice that I don't mention anything about monitoring the Outbound directory structure. I have struggled with this in the past, but have decided there is just no-good way to do this. You never really know when the trading partner will connect to your system and retrieve their files. When they do retrieve them, you don't know if they will delete them or leave them sitting out there for posterity. You can ask your trading partners to act in a certain way (and delete the files), and they may agree, but your convenience is not going to be a high priority for them.

Your use case, or business requirements, may be different and you want your monitoring process to check the outbound side of things as well. Using our example, you would just remove the condition that our process searches all directories underneath a directory named Inbound, and just search all directories and subdirectories from the starting point.

Processes

Now that you have a monitor process to check your directories for files, we need to have a way to make sure all of our processes are up and running. I am going to list two possible ways of doing this, although I am sure there are many more.

78 | DATA HERDING

1. Watch Process

You can create a process that will check all of your other processes are up and running. There are products you can purchase to do this, but creating one yourself is not difficult. It would look something like *figure 20*, below.

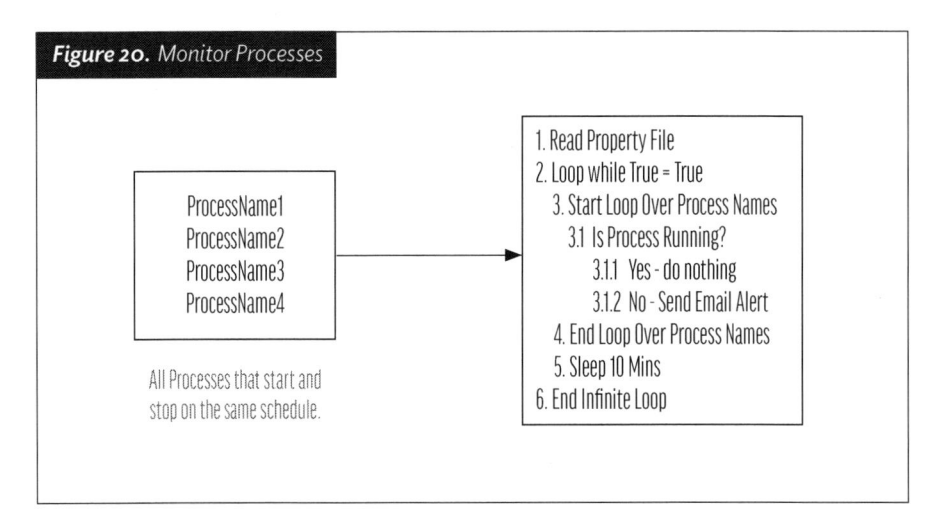

Figure 20. *Monitor Processes*

ProcessName1
ProcessName2
ProcessName3
ProcessName4

All Processes that start and stop on the same schedule.

1. Read Property File
2. Loop while True = True
3. Start Loop Over Process Names
   3.1 Is Process Running?
      3.1.1 Yes - do nothing
      3.1.2 No - Send Email Alert
4. End Loop Over Process Names
5. Sleep 10 Mins
6. End Infinite Loop

The property file will contain all of the process names that you want monitored. This will have to be maintained whenever you create a new process. This is one of those maintenance tasks that is easily overlooked, as mentioned before, but I don't see any way around this one. The Watch Process will be started up as a background process and will need to run on the same schedule as the processes it is monitoring. You don't want to be sending alerts when the process is in its normal down time.

If you have different processes that run on different schedules then you would have multiple Watch Processes running, and each property file would contain the process names that are all on the same schedule. So, you would have a property file that contains all of the process names that run 1:00 AM - 11:59 PM East Coast time in one property file, and another property file that contains all of the process names that run 1:00 AM - 11:59 PM West Coast time and it would feed its own separate copy of the Watch Process. The individual Watch Processes start and stop on the same schedule as the processes they are watching.

The sleep time in step 5 can be whatever you are comfortable with.

2. **Monitoring For Known File**

This is something that I have done when I had one "master file mover" on my server sitting in the DMZ, and one application sever that received the files and processed them. You could set up a test directory, on your file exchange server sitting in the DMZ, that your poller will pull from, and send the file to another test directory on your application server sitting in your core network. It would look something like the *figure 21*, below.

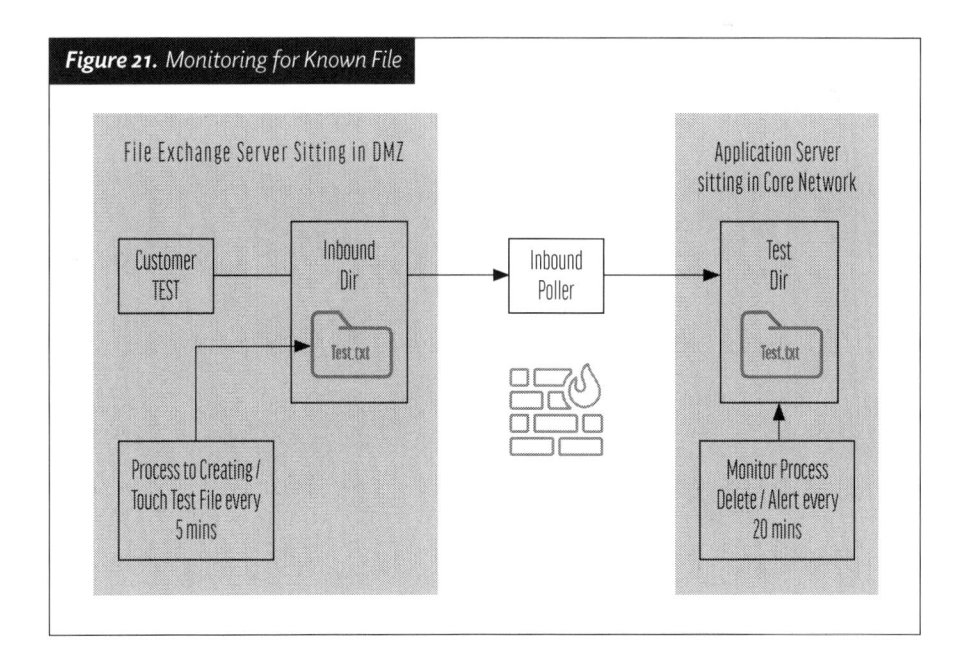

Figure 21. *Monitoring for Known File*

You have a process on your file exchange server that is creating a file, or touching a file, every 5 minutes. You are doing this because you don't want your file monitor process to be sending an alert that your test file is not being processed as it should. You also want to make sure that there will always be a file there for our purposes. When the test file is moved from the file exchange sever to your application server, you have another monitor process, on the application server, that is doing nothing but checking for the test file. If it sees the file then it will delete it, if it doesn't see the file then it will send an email alert because it knows that if there is no file then the polling process out in the DMZ is down. Once again, your "Delete/Alert monitor" will need to run on the same schedule as your polling process, because you don't want to send out an alert when there really should not be a file there.

Disk Space

I'm not sure it is the responsibility of the EDI group to monitor disk space, but you have to make sure that someone is doing it. Whenever a disk gets somewhere between 85 and 90 percent full, an alert needs to go out. If a disk runs out of space it has ripple effects throughout other systems, and none of them are good.

Disk usage could jump out of the norm for various reasons. If someone is doing a load test, that could have an effect. If you have recently on-boarded a new customer and they are sending a lot more files than you accounted for that could cause problems.

Connectivity

There should be a process that will connect to your file exchange server every so often (every hour or so), and send an alert if the connection fails.

> *"The single biggest problem in communication is the illusion that it has taken place."*
>
> *George Bernard Shaw*

06

> Email is a double-edged sword. We need it but it can consume us if we aren't careful. Having clear and concise messages will help keep you out ahead of problems.

> CHAPTER SIX

Emails and Alerts

We have already spoken about monitoring and sending alerts. For our purposes we are going to assume that the alerts being sent are via email. You need to think about your email strategy early on in your process. The one thing that you want to avoid is generating so many emails that important messages, things that you need to take action on, are missed or lost in the noise. This is very easy to do.

I've mentioned that you need to decide if you only want to send a message when an error is encountered or even when a file is processed successfully. I am intentionally avoiding making a recommendation because I feel there is benefit to both. By only sending alerts when there is an error you greatly reduce the amount of email traffic, but if you are also sending emails (informational) whenever a file is processed, it can be very helpful in finding things and answering questions about events that have happened in the past.

In this section I want to go over the different components of the email and things you need to think about.

Subject Line

Always include the environment in the subject line so you know if the event is taking place in production or test.

The subject line should let you know what has happened and where it has happened. Below are some sample subject lines:

- [PRODUCTION] Msg - Billing File Sent
- [PRODUCTION] ALERT - Failed to send Billing File
- [UAT] Msg - Payment File Received
- [UAT] ALERT - Failed to Decrypt Payment File

You should easily be able to scan your email and determine what has happened and what you need to act upon. You should know if an event has taken place in a test environment or the production environment. You should know if it is an error condition or just an informational message.

The environment (production, uat, dev, etc.) will need to be a variable that is set depending on where your code is running. You don't want to have to manually adjust this as the code moves from one environment to the next. The main text of the subject line will be situational specific.

You could create two different email subject line variables that would look something like this:

ALERT_SUBJ = [$environment$] ALERT -
MSG_SUBJ= [$environment$] Msg -

You would then just append the "situational specific" detail at the end of the appropriate subject line variable. Append to the end of

$ALERT_SUBJ if it is an error condition, or $MSG_SUBJ if it is just an informational message.

To Address

You need to have at least three different levels of "To addresses" for sending emails.

- o Dev Group - Emails that are generated in the non-production environments should be sent to this group. This group should contain the developers that are actually building and testing the code. Not only do they need to know that the code is doing what is expected, they need to see the emails to make sure they are correct and contain all of the necessary information.

- o Support Group - Emails should be sent to this group only from the production environment, and it should only contain the people that are responsible to act on an event. If it is an error condition then this should be the people that will determine what the exact problem is and act accordingly. It is the same people that would receive a request from the business unit like "I need to you re-send the billing file from Customer ABC that we got last Thursday".

- o Business Unit - You should never send an email to the business unit from a non-production environment. Even though it will say that it is from [DEVELOPMENT] trust me, it will only create confusion. There will be some business units that are very sensitive to files coming and going between them and the external customer. They may want to be copied in on all informational as well as error emails. There will probably be situations where the back-end process is manual, and the business unit needs to know when a file has arrived so they know they need to act upon it.

You should avoid like the plaque the urge and the constant requests to add an individual to an email. If you do this then you will constantly be removing and adding people to and from the emails as their roles change and as they move into and out of the company. It should be required that the code only contain distribution lists. And it is the responsibility of the individual user to be added to the correct list. You need to be able to tell them what list they need to be added to, but it should be up to them to get that done.

On the other hand, if you are forced to use individual names it could bring up some good nostalgia when you are looking through some code, or receiving one of the emails. *"Oh yeah, that person. They haven't been here in over six years. I wonder what they are up to now."*

Email Body

The body of the email should contain all necessary details to locate and resolve the problem.

- The name of the file
  * I have seen some instances where the file is actually attached to the email.
- Where the error occurred
  * The name of the event, the program name, the procedure name, the step name. Whatever it is that will allow you to know exactly where the error happened.
- The actual error itself

* Stack trace, error code and description. Whatever the system returns for the error condition.

Rules vs Chaos

No matter how you choose to implement your email/alert notification process, you are probably going to need to create some rules to help maintain some level of sanity.

The first rule I would recommend is to make any production error alert stand out. In keeping with the example we have been working with you could create a rule that says:

- Subject containing "[PRODUCTION] ALERT" mark as important and change color to red. So, by scanning your inbox you would see something like this
  * ! [PRODUCTION] ALERT - Failed to send Billing File

Whatever you decide to do, you just need to do something that makes a production error stand out and get noticed. This is something that someone needs to act on as soon as possible in order to avoid bringing unwanted attention to the EDI group.

If you have decided to send informational messages then I would recommend creating folders that are situational specific. For example, creating a folder with a name like EDI_Billing, then create a rule

- Subject containing "[PRODUCTION] Msg - Billing File Sent" move to folder EDI_Billing.

You may wind up with a lot of folders and a lot of rules, but when it comes time to find something your search area will be narrowed down. You can choose to get as detailed or as general as you feel comfortable with.

The downside of sending emails directly to folders is that if someone does a "reply" to the email with some information that you need to see, the rule will automatically route it to your folder instead of to your inbox. You may not know that the message was ever sent until the person reaches out to you.

You will need to decide how to handle emails from non-production environments. I generally just send them to my trash. If you do this, however, you need to remember that if you are testing your own code, you need to look in the trash folder for the emails that the code is generating.

Should alerts go to a dedicated in-box, or to a distribution list

When emails are sent by the system should they go to a particular in-box that is being monitored, or does it go to a distribution list so it is delivered to several people at once.

Distribution group

- *Pros*
    - A lot of people will see the message at the same time
    - You don't have to be looking at multiple in-boxes
- *Cons*
    - Generates more email
    - More than one person may act on the email
        * Wasted effort
        * Customer could get confused having multiple contacts

Specific In-box
- *Pros*
  - Less email generated
- *Cons*
  - Have to be looking at multiple in-boxes
  - Message could get over looked
    * Person assigned to monitor for errors is out or not available.
  - Rules created for handling the email will need to be done by committee instead of each individual having the luxury of handling them like they want.

I personally like the email going to a distribution group. I just don't like having to monitor multiple in-boxes.

Email is a double-edged sword. We need it but it can consume us if we aren't careful. Having clear and concise messages will help keep you out ahead of problems.

07

> You should always ask questions about how the other team is processing the data, and try to think things through. Don't count on people on the other side of the boundary to understand how things like this should work..

> CHAPTER SEVEN

Boundaries

A boundary is a definite place where your responsibility ends and someone else's begins. It stops you from doing things for others that they should do for themselves.

When you are dealing with data flowing between your system and an external customer's system, it is pretty clear that is in the "EDI space". Once the data is within your organization, however, it can become fuzzy where your responsibility ends and someone else's begins. We have discussed transforming the data from one form into another. Sometimes that is done by the EDI team but sometimes it isn't.

Where to place the boundaries of what is an EDI service and what isn't, has no hard and fast rules, and it will probably be different in different use cases. One thing I can guarantee you, however, is that no matter what everyone agrees to, you will be dragged into many situations where the only thing you can say is "see the other person". It doesn't matter how many times you have to explain to the same person or persons that once the file makes it to a certain point you are out of the picture, they will still come to you. You just need to take a breath, keep calm, and direct them to the person who can help resolve their problem.

92 | DATA HERDING

In computer systems, just like in geopolitics, where you have boundaries there is going to be conflict. This is where your archives are going to be of great benefit to you. But there can also be issues around processing and the sequencing of events. I can give you one example of a situation I have been involved with. My system was responsible for simply taking a file that a customer had uploaded to one of our servers and moving it to a location where another system would transform the file. Then my system would take the transformed file and move it to another location to be ingested by a back-end process. Sounds simple enough, and all we had to do was agree on the locations for drop off and pickup.

The team that was responsible for doing the data transformation, however, was taking the file we dropped off for them, moved it to the location that we were supposed to pickup the transformed file from, and then did the transformation in that location. Below *(figure 22)*, is a sequence diagram of how things were set up. The processes in the top half of the diagram are EDI processes, and the processes in the bottom half, and in between the dark lines, belong to the other business unit.

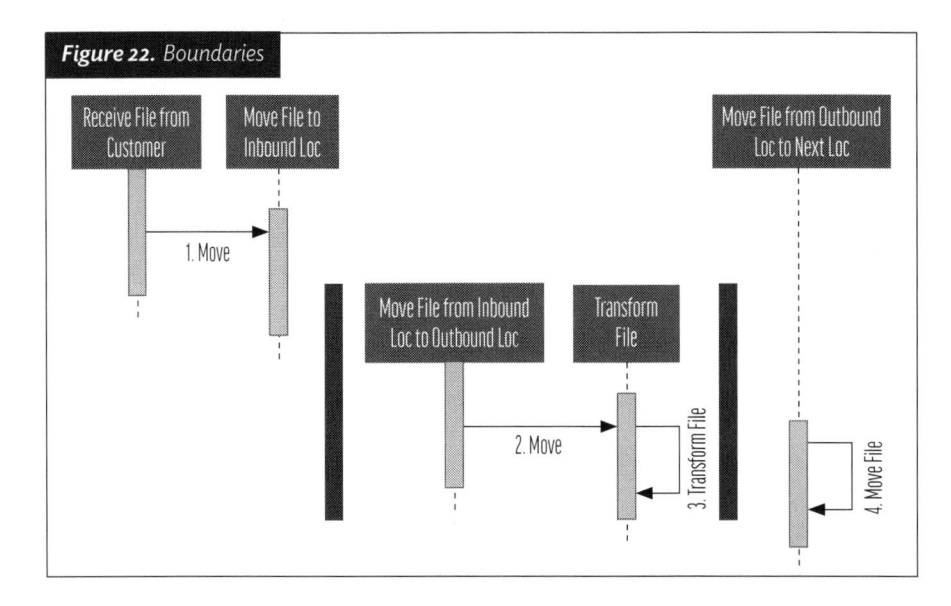

Figure 22. Boundaries

I think you can spot the problem here right away. Our polling process (step 4) was very frequent to provide good customer service. As soon as the un-transformed file was placed in the outbound location, we picked it up and moved it on down the line before the transform even had a chance to take place.

The correct answer here is to not place the file in the outbound location until after it has been transformed and ready to go. The other team could have simply done the transform in the first location before moving the file; or moved the file to a temporary location, done the transform, and moved the file to the outbound location. Once we identified the problem and met with the other team to discuss the issue, the response we got was this:

"Oh no we can't do that. We would have to go back and re-design our entire process and this has to work now. You figure it out and we will make a note that we need to make the change you have requested. We will add this to our backlog but we can't commit to when it will get done."

So, to try to be accommodating and to meet the needs of the business we came up with an esoteric polling schedule. We made the move to the inbound location (step 1) run at the top of the hour, and the move to the next system (step 4), run at thirty minutes after the hour. Of course, then we had introduced unnecessary complexity into our system. When things go wrong in the future, as you know they will, it will take forever to figure out these dependencies.

Once the timing solution was in place, the process change that needed to happen with the other system never occurred. I'm sure that is a huge surprise to no one.

I'm not trying to say that I have an answer for things like this. I'm just trying to make you aware that stuff like this is going to happen; a lot. You should always ask questions about how the other team is processing the data, and try to think things through. Don't count on people on the other side of the boundary to understand how things like this should work. This isn't something they have to deal with on a daily basis, and they will generally take the shortest path from point A to point B without thinking through the consequences.

If someone throws a fit because you set a boundary, it is just more evidence that a boundary is needed.

08

> Make certain your systems are well documented. As your systems change make sure that the documentation is kept up to date.

> CHAPTER EIGHT

Common Pitfalls

Despite your best intentions and plans, it is certain that something at some point will need troubleshooting. In this section I go over the most common issues that I have come across.

How many times are you going to send me that same file

One thing that I have seen happen over and over is processing the same file over and over (see what I did there). Once you process a file it is important that something is done with the file to prevent it from being processed again. Usually this depends on where you are accessing the file. You will either be accessing it on an internal server, or an external customers server. If the file is on your internal server then you would normally want to move it to an archive area once you have successfully processed it. If it is on an external customer's server, then you would probably want to delete the file once you have successfully retrieved it to your server. You will have to work with your trading partner to make sure that you have delete permission on the files you are accessing.

I have created interfaces to external systems where I am retrieving files and have not been allowed to delete them. In these situations, you will have to get clever on how to determine which files to process and which ones to leave alone. You will need to have a way to determine which files you have processed and which ones you haven't. You can do this either by using file names, date time stamps, file content, or some combination of these things. This can get complicated pretty quickly depending on how often you are polling your trading partner. If it is just once a day, or once a month, time stamps may be sufficient. If you are polling multiple times a day then your best bet may be to do a checksum of the files content. You would calculate the checksum of the file on the external server, and then compare it to the checksums of the files already retrieved to your server. The number of files on your server that you would need to check for a duplicate would dictate how you would implement such a solution. If you have only a few files then you could do it on the fly, if you could have many files then you would want to store the checksums in a data base table and do a query so your processing time could be kept to a minimum.

It is not safe to use the logic that my system polls the customer's server every hour, so if I see a file that is over an hour old sitting on their server then I can ignore it. Suppose there is a network issue that prevents you from polling the external server for three hours. If there were files created an hour into the outage, then when your process re-connects it would see those files as being two hours old and it would ignore them.

The one thing you don't want to have happen is to process the same files over and over. Depending on what is happening with the files on the back-end processes, it could have a large impact on the business (processing the same order for a customer over and over). At the same time, you have to be sure you are processing all of the files that you are supposed to or there will be a business impact with that as well, for example, not getting customer orders.

Where the heck are all of the files the customer sent

There are a lot of reasons that you may not process files that a customer has sent you. One of the things that comes to my mind is I had established an interface with an external customer and we had agreed upon a file naming-convention. We were using PGP encryption and the file extension we had both agreed to was "pgp". We tested, brought the interface up, and files were going back and forth for an extended period of time. One day, for whatever reason, the customer started sending files with an extension of PGP (all upper case). Since our poller was set up looking for files with an extension of pgp the files stopped being processed and started to just stack up in the inbound directory on our server. Nobody noticed anything until the internal business unit started asking questions about why they had not received files from this particular customer, which was unusual. The reason nobody noticed, and the business unit got involved, is because there was no directory monitor at the time. This brought unwanted attention to the EDI group and was considered a failure on our part.

There are a lot of other reasons files may not be processed:
- Your file polling process could be down
- There could be an issue with the external customer's system where they are not sending you files and you need to bring it to their attention. This happens more times than you would expect. Letting them know they have a problem before they know about it is providing good customer service.
  * There was one type of file that was critical to an internal business process. If the business did not receive the files from the vendor then the automated processing of orders got diverted to a manual process and could bring things to a crawl. From an

EDI perspective there was really no way of knowing that we did not receive files that some other business unit was expecting. After this happened a couple of times, we looked at the traffic to determine how things looked when everything was working. It could be seen that when things got started in the mornings, they were receiving batches of files every ten minutes. It was decided to create a monitor on the archive area for these files. The monitor would start on the days of the week and at the time that business would normally start. If the monitor did not see a file for thirty minutes then it would start sending out alerts. The alert would contain the amount of time since the last file was received. When we received an alert, we would contact the vendor, and they were made aware of an issue on their side before they were aware of it.

- Someone could have altered things on your server without you even knowing
  * Changed permissions
  * Disabled accounts
  * Upgraded an operating system that is causing things to work differently
- The external trading partner starts doing something different for no apparent reason

Some of these things, of course, are out of your control. But as I mentioned earlier you will be blamed for the failures no matter what.

There are things you can do to try to alleviate some of these issues.

- Don't make your file naming conventions case specific when setting up your polling processes.
- Monitor directories for files older than some period of time
  * If you know that any file that comes into a particular directory should be processed within an hour, then send an alert if you find any files older than three hours in that directory.
    - There are third party products to do this, but creating one yourself is not difficult.
- Monitor processes
  * If there are processes that should be running have a "watch" that checks for the process and sends an alert if the process is down.
    - There are third party products to do this, but creating one yourself is not difficult.
- Monitor the server itself
  * Have a process that makes a connection to your server to make sure it can successfully login.
    - Send an alert of the connection fails.

How come we did not get all of the files

I have seen situations where a process will work fine when it is processing one file at a time, but fail when it is processing a large number of files. This can be due to several different reasons. One that I want to discuss here is file naming. A lot of times, in order to create uniqueness in a file name, a date-time stamp will be added to the name of the file.

As long as there is one file everything is fine. If there are multiple files being processed in a short period of time, however, and your naming convention just goes down to the minute; then you are guaranteed to create files with the same name, thus overwriting some files in the process.

If you are using date time stamps to avoid overwriting files then you should use the smallest time increment in your filename that your system allows. You can usually get to milli-second or a thousandth of a second. You should also introduce a delay of a second or more, if possible, when moving files from one place to another. If your time stamp for your file naming convention goes to the milli-second, and you have a delay of one second between naming the files, then that should be enough to guarantee unique filenames and prevent the overwriting of files. If your time stamp can only get down to the second, then introduce a delay of two seconds and that should do the trick.

Overwriting, or losing, files is another negative business impact thing that will bring unwanted attention to you and your team.

Folklore

Make certain your systems are well documented. As your systems change make sure that the documentation is kept up to date. Make certain that the location of the documentation is known to everyone and that it is easy to get to, and insist that all responsible parties read it and stay current on everything. All of these things are good advice. I also know it is the same as telling you to eat right and exercise regularly. We all know it is the right thing to do. But life just gets in the way.

I have been working in the financial services sector for the past eighteen years. There has been a lot of upheaval during that time to say the least. I want to bring out one example to help illustrate the point I am trying to make. There is one particular company that has changed names four different times during those eighteen years. I think once was when the division I interfaced with was spun off into its own company. Then it was bought and sold a couple of times. I think there was a re-branding effort thrown in there somewhere along the way. From my perspective, however, it was always the same company and we were always sending the same data back and forth to each other.

On our back-end system that just crunches the data, a system that hasn't changed much in the past forty years, it is still referenced as the first name the company ever had. The directory that the trading partner sends its files to has the third name of the company. Where those files are being archived, however, has the second name. Anything that has been created over the past couple of years with this trading partner has the fourth name of the company associated with it. Whatever name the company had at the time we were working with them, is the name associated with that particular work product.

When someone new comes onto this team to work, they are easily confused by things like this. I get that. If you haven't been around for a long time you just don't understand all of the nuances about the business. I am not the one that coined the term folklore for things like this, but I think it is a good description. It is things that are just inside people's heads. It is not written down anywhere. Sometimes it is stuff like this that makes people run away screaming never wanting to work in the EDI space ever again.

I wish I had a solution I could give you to solve this problem. I would write a book and become rich and famous. I know things like this are not unique to the EDI space, but I think it is probably more pronounced in our area because we are interfacing with our external customers. Our set of customers is always changing, and they are always changing how they do things. Some companies that we think are going to become our customer, and we put in time and effort to build interfaces with, never become our customer at all. Their priorities change, they decide to go with a competitor, they go out of business, or some other reason they just decide to do something else. One particular trading partner I was working with one time actually got raided by the Feds, and the principals of the company sent to jail. Now you will have code, directories, accounts, and interfaces that will never be used. Who has the time to go back and clean all of that stuff up?

New Person: "I didn't even know we did business with company ABC."
You: "We don't."
New Person (Looking at an account with the name CompanyABC): "Oh...okay."

09

> You should really do a test to see what kind of issues you are going to have with the data set. Remember I said earlier that no one implements a data standard in a standard way.

> CHAPTER NINE

The Reason for Consistency

NOW IS THE TIME THAT we are going to try and put everything together into one smooth operating system.

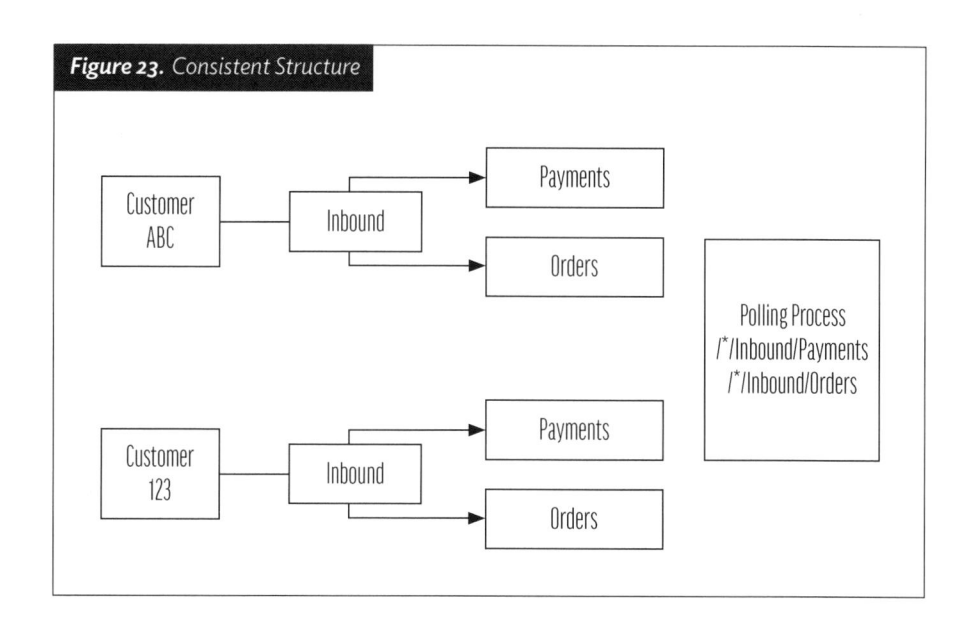

Figure 23. Consistent Structure

In the *figure 23* above, I am depicting a pretty simple file exchange system. We have a server with two external user accounts with identical directory structures. We are going to assume that we are using industry standards for both the format and the data for our inbound files. We have a polling process looking for inbound payment and order files.

Now suppose that we have a third customer that wants to set up electronic payments and orders with us. If we have a script that we can execute that will create an account and directory structure; then all we have to do is run that script, send the credentials to our new trading partner, and we are done.

If we have fought the good fight and convinced our new customer to use industry standards, and we have convinced them to use our preferred directory structure, our life is easy. I actually believe that I have had this scenario play out one or two times in my illustrious career. If it happened every time, or even once-in-a-while, then we would be living in that fictional Nirvana world that I mentioned earlier.

Hopefully your new trading partner will want to test with you before implementing the new connection in production. Hopefully your new trading partner has a test system (hopefully you do). You should really do a test to see what kind of issues you are going to have with the data set. *Remember I said earlier that no one implements a data standard in a standard way.* You are probably going to need to make a few tweaks to your data mapping for their "unique business needs". But your level of effort in on-boarding your new customer will be much less by virtue of you having a consistent directory structure, and you and your trading partner using standards.

If your trading partner does something wrong, for example, places an order file in the Payments directory then your monitoring is going to alert you to the issue and you will get it sorted out before anyone notices that the order hasn't arrived.

10

> Do not offer any information that is not directly requested and don't do anything to try and "help" the auditor with their job. They know what their job is and it is incumbent upon them to know what questions to ask and to ask them.

>CHAPTER TEN

People, Places and Things

You may have noticed that for a book about technology I've talked a lot about people: your trading partners, internal customers, colleagues. And I've talked a lot about how things can get lost in translation, or actually not get said at all and this frustrates the EDI process. All of the years working in this field has taught me that if standards are the foundation, to return to Chapter 1, then having good relationships, time for people, and fostering open communications is the bedrock for setting up and managing good EDI.

The unexpected

There will be some situations that you will come across that you will not be prepared for, and they will come at you out of nowhere. One particular example that I want to share with you happened to me when I was helping to implement a new distribution system in a warehouse in Ireland. I was going around meeting the different people in the warehouse when I came across an elderly man that was having problems with the new scale application that had just been installed. It was a pretty simple interface but the issue was that he had never used a computer before, much less a mouse. I got him to demonstrate the issue he was having and this is what I saw. He would gingerly take the mouse by its sides and position it over the field or button that he needed to click. He would then remove his hand, and using only his index finger he would firmly poke the mouse button. This would of course cause the mouse to move off of the field or button, and was causing him endless frustration.

I had already implemented this same system in several warehouses in the US, and I thought I had seen every issue that anyone could have with it, but I admit that I was totally unprepared and wasn't sure how to react to what I was seeing. Even after showing him, and putting my hand over his and demonstrating how to control the mouse I'm not sure he ever got the hang of it. I believe they had to find him another position until he eventually retired.

Keeping with the same Ireland trip I want to relate another situation that I was totally unprepared for. The manufacturing facility for the company was in the Republic of Ireland, but the distribution facility was in Northern Ireland. My trip was in the late 1990's so it was several years after the official ending of "The Troubles", but with so many people having been killed during the conflict there was still a lot of tension between Northern Ireland and the Republic of Ireland.

Most of my work was in the distribution facility and I spent the majority of my time there training the people and installing the new system. One of the process changes in the warehouse was once an order was picked and staged on the shipping floor, someone needed to scan the bar-code on each individual box. This did a lot of things system wise:

- It validated that the order was complete and ready to go.
- If there was something missing from the order, or there was something there that should not be, then it would let them know so they could correct it.
- If the order needed to be changed prior to shipping that could be done as well.
  - If the customer called requesting that something be added or removed it could easily be done with a few scans.
  - If a "more important" customer needed something that was not in inventory, but was on the staged order, it could be removed from the staged order and shipped to the other customer.

All of the checks were done instantly, and all changes were updated in the database in real time. It was a good system if I say so myself. It saved a lot of time, wasted effort, and prevented mistakes being made on the orders.

One evening when I was in a pub (you can't work all the time) one of the guys I had worked with from the warehouse came over, sat down, and bought me a whiskey. They are friendly people and it would have been rude of me not to accept his offer. He began to tell me his concern he had about the scan they were going to have to do after each order was staged. He was convinced this was going to add several hours of time to every order and it was just not possible to accomplish. In reality if he had to completely load the largest truck they had, with the smallest boxes in the warehouse, he could accomplish the scanning in about eight minutes maximum. We went round and round for several minutes trying to convince each other of our point of view. Finally, he told me what his real concern was.

He said "Keet". There is no "th" sound in the Irish dialect so Keith becomes Keet (three becomes tree but that is another story all-together).

He said "Keet, you don't understand. They want us to fail. The people down in the Republic want to prove that we can't do our jobs. They want to shut down the whole operation here and move everything down there. They hate us so much, but we just want to do our jobs and do them well. They are making us do this scan to guarantee we won't get the orders out on time."

Since I was the main designer and developer of this warehouse system, I knew this was not true. I also knew that I could not disregard or make fun of what he was saying. I did not understand the political history of the area, but I could tell that he was sincere in what he was saying and what he believed. I simply had to say that if this became a problem then I would personally figure out a system work around.

I'm sure you will never come across these exact scenarios. However, I promise you will come across things that will make you equally as surprised, as these were for me. I know that making money is the main goal of any business, but I think it is important that you not lose sight of the fact that people are the most important thing. How you get along with people is much more important than how you get along with a computer system.

Having just made the comment that people are the most important thing, I want to mention something else that I personally struggle with. If you work in technology, rather it be EDI or any other area, we are generally working on some sort of automation and trying to make things more efficient. This potentially has the side effect of making some people redundant and results in job loss. I know that I have worked on projects that have resulted in other people losing their job. Sometimes this is how progress is defined. I'm not sure that I have any advice on how to deal with this, but just like everything else I have mentioned here, I just want you to know that it is something that you need to be aware of.

I'm just the delivery person

Here is a typical conversation that you may want to have with one of your business users, but probably should not.

Business Unit Person: "Customer ABC is having a problem with their bill."
You: "Yeah, so."
Business Unit Person: "It is an EDI bill not a paper bill."
You: "Yeah, so."
Business Unit Person: "You are EDI, aren't you?"
You: "Yeah, so."
Business Unit Person: "You have to fix it and get them a good bill."
You: "Just like the last 136 times we have had this same conversation; I don't create the bill! I just deliver it to the customer! Now go away and leave me alone!"

Unfortunately, there is just no getting around this. Trust me, I have tried. Your job description mandates that you constantly straddle interfaces between systems. If you do your job well, and provide good friendly customer service to your internal business units, then they are going to come to you when they have a problem, regardless if you can do anything to help them or not. You need to have a contact list of the correct people you can direct them to. You also need to provide an explanation of why that person can help them instead of you. It may work every once in a while, and they will reach out to the correct person instead of you, but since you are interfacing with so many different business units, and people are constantly moving in and out of jobs, you will always be dealing with this. You just need to consider this as a standard part of your job description.

Fixing data issues

There will be situations where your customer, or trading partner, is doing something wrong. And a decision will have to be made if you ask the customer to correct the error, or you make an "adjustment" on your side.

A perfect example of this happened when the company I was working with started getting authentication failures from multiple customers. The reason for this was they were sending leading and/or trailing spaces in the username and/or password. Due to the authentication error, we could not process their orders. We did reach out to the customers about this, but since the situation was hurting business, and it was a trivial fix for us to make (just trimming any whitespace from the username and password) it was decided that we would implement the change on our side to allow the business to flow.

It is difficult to know how the error happened. I suspect, since both the username and password were pretty cryptic, that it was just a cut and paste error when the customer was entering the info into their system. Make no mistake about doing this, once you have made the allowance on your side, the customer will never make the correction on their end.

This is a gray area, and something I struggle with. This was a very real error, and if this was something internal to your own company you would insist that it be corrected. When dealing with a customer that pays you money, however, it is a little different. You need to straddle a line between providing good customer service, and maintaining your systems.

If the customer sends bad data, but you know how to fix it, do you do this or let the customer know and have them resend it. There could be legal repercussions if you alter the data received directly from a customer. At the same time, it could be the end of the quarter and orders need to be processed so people get paid their commissions properly. Once again something like this should be a policy decision made at the management level. It could be a different decision based on the situation. This is something you need to think about and plan for ahead of time so you will know how to react when the situation happens. And trust me it will happen.

Auditing

If you ever find yourself lucky enough to be involved with an audit, I can give you a few words of advice. Never answer a question unless it is specifically directed to you. A lot of times the auditors, either internal or external, will just throw a question out there not directed to anyone in particular just to see who will answer. Don't be afraid of "dead air" or feel compelled to jump in when no one else will.

When you do answer a question, your prime directive should be to answer with either "yes" or "no". If that is not possible, then you should use the least number of words as possible to answer the exact question asked. Do not elaborate or try to provide clarity for them. If they ask the wrong question it is not your responsibility to either correct them or point it out to them. When answering a question make sure you answer truthfully. If you don't know the answer don't be afraid to say so, but make sure to find the answer and follow up in a timely manner.

Usually when auditors are looking at IT systems they are interested in policies and procedures. They want to make sure they exists, they are documented, and that they are being followed. They will also be interested in security. They will want to know if encryption is used, what type of encryption, and the when, where and how it is implemented. They will want to know retention policies of data and log files, and who has access. Make sure you have this information available, or the people who know these things are available.

You should not do anything to make an audit adversarial, believe me that is in no one's best interests. But do not offer any information that is not directly requested and don't do anything to try and "help" the auditor with their job. They know what their job is and it is incumbent upon them to know what questions to ask and to ask them.

Helpful hint: If you give verbal responses, if possible, follow-up after your conversation with an email to (1) clarify what was discussed; and (2) have your own documentation of the discussion. Furthermore, if the auditor has concerns with your written description, they should follow-up immediately.

Disaster Recovery

I have heard this referred to as both disaster recovery and business recovery. Whatever you call it, it refers to bringing up an alternative system because your primary system has had some sort of failure.

- Loss of power
  * Construction - Line is cut
  * Storm - Takes out power lines and transformers
- Hardware
  * Breaks - Mechanical failure of some kind
  * Incompatibility - Something new has been installed and causes failures
  * Configuration - Some change is made to settings which causes failures
- Software
  * Third Party - Purchased software starts throwing an error
  * Incompatibility - New software has been installed and is causing failures
  * Internal Glitch - Software developed internally starts to cause failures
- Communication
  * Vendor - Your comm vendor has internal failure
  * Constriction - Line is cut
  * Storm - Takes out communication lines

I have seen all of the above situations occur at one time or another. There should be a plan in place to recover from any of the above. The plan can be as elaborate as having multiple data centers scattered geographically around the world, or as simple as having off-site backups of your systems.

There should also be a plan to practice the recovery of your system for when something does happen. You don't want to discover a weakness in the plan when you are in the middle of an actual emergency. The practice plan can happen in a number of different ways.

- Bring up a parallel system just for test
  * As long as the parallel system is not available to your trading partners you don't really need to worry about any impact to them.

- Bring up a parallel system for test but "swing the network".
  * In this scenario your test system will be available to your trading partners and you need to include them in your test planning.
    - Make sure you communicate to all of your trading partners not to transmit data during the time frame of your test.
    - Since you know your communication will be ignored, you should go the extra step to make sure all of the accounts for your trading partners are disabled. This way when they eventually do send production data during your test, they will get an error and they know they need to keep trying to send the data.
    - There should be at least one account available on the parallel test system that you, or the testers, have access to so the EDI precesses can be validated. But this account should not be accessible to any of your trading partners.

We have come to the end of our journey through EDI. I hope that you were able to learn a thing or two. And I hope that your data gets where it needs to go in a timely and efficient manner. Perhaps these are the most important lessons of all:

- *EDI is more about people, than people realize. remember that and be humble.*
- *If you're everyone's go-to problem solver, then take that as a compliment.*
- *Sometimes good business means writing logic that you'd really rather not, but it's not always your call.*

> ACKNOWLEDGMENTS

Writing a book is a lot harder than I ever thought it would be. Even without a world-wide pandemic raging. There are so many people that have mentored me, helped me, and encouraged me over time; and I feel indebted to them all.

There are a few people that I want to call out by name. First would have to be my wife Patti. She has been my partner in everything for over twenty-five years. Nothing I have done or accomplished would have been possible without her.

I want to thank Mike Fleck. He is the one that hired me into the "EDI world" so many years ago and took me under his wing. We had a heck-of-a-ride together.

Lastly, I want to thank Cindy Yuan. When I felt so many things were up in the air for me, she made me feel like a valued person for my depth of knowledge.

> THANK YOU

*Thank you sincerely for reading this book.
I hope you have found the information useful.
I hope you will leave a review rather you liked it or not.*

>KEEP IN TOUCH

If you would like to stay in touch and hear more about what I have to say about the EDI world, and things in general, you can browse over to my web site and look through some of the blog posts. You can also sign up and get a notification when new content is published.

https://www.thedataherder.com

> APPENDIX

Terms

AS2 – Applicability Statement 2 - A secure way of sending files between servers. It allows for the sender of the file to request a Message Disposition Notification (MDN)

Business unit – A group of people, internal to your company, that you provide a service to.

DMZ – Demilitarized Zone. An area of a network that is behind a firewall facing a public network (the internet), and in front of a firewall protecting the core network of an organization.

EDI – Electronic Data Interchange. The process of exchanging data with another system. You will hear others define EDI as the transmission of X12 data sets between trading partners. For the purposes of this book, I choose to define it more broadly. It could be exchanging data with a trading partner (external customer), or another business unit within your own organization.

FTP – File Transfer Protocol. A non-secure protocol for sending files between servers.

FTPS – File Transfer Protocol Secure. A secure protocol for sending files between servers. If you establish communications between the servers using port 20, then an explicit command must be issued in order to send the file securely (Explicit Encryption). Else the file transmission is the same as FTP. If you establish communications between the servers using port 990, then no command needs to be given (Implicit Encryption)

HTTP - Hypertext Transfer Protocol. A non-secure way to browse and send file on the internet.

HTTPS - Hypertext Transfer Protocol Secure. A secure way to browse and send files on the internet.

IP - Internet Protocol. A set of rules that dictate how data should be delivered over the public internet.

IP Address - Internet Protocol Address. A numerical label designed to each device connected to a computer network that uses the internet protocol for communication.

MDN - Message Disposition Notification. An acknowledgment that can be requested by the sender of a message sent over the AS2 protocol. It is sent after the file has been successfully decrypted by the receiver. This provides the sender with legal proof that the message (or file) was successfully delivered without being altered in transit.

Monitor - A process that is checking for an anomalous condition. For example, a file sitting in a directory longer than it should

PGP - Pretty Good Privacy. Used for encrypting and decrypting data.

Polling - A process that is checking a certain location or locations for files to be moved or processed.

Server - A piece of hardware that a system runs on.

Servicer - An entity that sits between your system and your trading partner. Your outbound traffic flows from your system to the servicer, and then from the servicer to your trading partner. Your inbound traffic flows from your external trading partner to the servicer, and then from the servicer to your system.

SFTP - SSH File Transfer Protocol (most people will refer to this as Secure FTP). A secure protocol for sending files between servers.

SSH - Secure Shell. A cryptographic network protocol for operating network services securely over an unsecured network.

System - Software that provides a business function.

Trading partner - Trading partner and external customer are synonymous. This is someone that you exchange data with.

White Listing - A security feature often used for limiting access only to trusted users.

XML - Extensible Markup Language. A defined standard used for encoding documents in a format that is both human-readable and machine-readable.

Note: People will use polling and monitoring interchangeably. I'm making a distinction to avoid confusion in the text of this book.

Questionnaire

When you are on-boarding a new customer, there are certain details that need to be covered. I've tried to capture what those are and placed them in the form of a questionnaire below.

1. Host Info - Trading partner server
    1.1. Host name and IP Test
    1.2. Host name and IP Production
    1.3. Host name and IP Recovery

2. Host Info - Your server
    2.1. Host name and IP Test
    2.2. Host name and IP Production
    2.3. Host name and IP Recovery

3. Credentials - Your server
    3.1. Username/Password Test
    3.2. Username/Password Production
    3.3. SSH key used
    3.4. SSL certificates needed for signing

4. Credentials - Trading partner server
    4.1. Username/Password Test
    4.2. Username/Password Production
    4.3. SSH key used
    4.4. SSL certificates needed for signing

5. Encryption
    5.1. Encryption used
    5.2. Different keys for different environments
    5.3. Key exchange

6. Direction of data flow
    6.1. Customer pushes data to your host
    6.2. You push data to customer's host
    6.3. Customer polls your host for data
    6.4. You poll customers host for data

7. Directory structure
    7.1. Directory structure on your host
    7.2. Directory structure on trading partner's host

8. Down time or maintenance windows
    8.1. Customer's host test
    8.2. Customer's host prod
    8.3. Your host test
    8.4. Your host prod

Made in the USA
Columbia, SC
14 May 2022